Balm From Beyond

By the same author

Buried Alive: Horrors of the Undead
Disembodied Voices
Doubles: The Enigma of the Second Self
Journeys to Heaven and to Hell
Supernatural Disappearances

Balm From Beyond

HOW THE DEPARTED CAN HELP US

Rodney Davies

ROBERT HALE · LONDON

© Rodney Davies 2010
First published in Great Britain 2010

ISBN 978-0-7090-8951-3

Robert Hale Limited
Clerkenwell House
Clerkenwell Green
London EC1R 0HT

www.halebooks.com

The right of Rodney Davies
to be identified as author of this work has been
asserted by him in accordance with the
Copyright, Designs and Patents Act 1988

All illustrations by Rodney Davies

A catalogue record for this book is available from the British Library

2 4 6 8 10 9 7 5 3 1

Typeset in 10.5/13.5pt Sabon
Printed in Great Britain by the MPG Books Group,
Bodmin and King's Lynn

Shall we disdain their silent, soft address;
Their posthumous Advice, and pious pray'er?
Senseless, as Herds that graze their hallow'd Graves,
Tread underfoot their Agonies and Groans,
Frustrate their Anguish, and destroy their Deaths?

from *The Complaint; or, Night Thoughts on Life,*
Death and Immortality by Edward Young

ACKNOWLEDGEMENTS

I thank all those who so kindly gave up their time to talk to me about their experience of being contacted by the dead.

Extracts from the copyrighted materials shown below are reprinted by permission of the publishers:

Robson Books, London, UK
p.38, 'The Ghost in the Bedroom' by John Blashford-Snell, from *Ghostly Encounters* by Astrid St Aubyn, with Zahra Hanbury (Robson Books, London, 1998)

The Society for Psychical Research
pp.59–60, 89–90, *Proceedings*, Volume XXXIII
p.98, 'Extraordinary Experiences of the Bereaved' by Louis E. LaGrand, PhD, from *The Psi Researcher*, November 1996
p.197, 'A Costermonger's Comforting Mongrel' by Margaret Moreham, from *The Psi Researcher*, November 1995
p.200, 'A Feline Ghost in Double Vision' by Riftah Brown, from *The Paranormal Review*, April 1999
pp.203–204, 'A Disappearing Village and Coach' by Michael Higgins, from *The Psi Researcher*, February 1996

Nimbus Publishing, Nova Scotia, Canada
pp.88, 102, 130, 142, *Bluenose Ghosts* by Helen Creighton (Nimbus Publishing, 1994)

Every effort has been made to contact all copyright holders. My apologies are offered if any oversights or omissions have occurred. The publisher would be pleased to rectify these in future editions.

Contents

List of Illustrations   8

Introduction   9

1   Dabbling with Doubles   12

2   Wraiths and Ghosts   27

3   The Departed Make Contact   42

4   Unseen Impressions   72

5   Odours and Faces   81

6   Voices and Other Sounds   90

7   Mists and Vapours   100

8   Easing a Broken Heart   116

9   Contact through Dreams   129

10   The Wraith as Crime Solver   146

11   Souls in Crisis   157

12   Animals, Cars and Aircraft   181

13   More Strange Happenings   207

Bibliography   220

Index   222

List of Illustrations

Figure

1. Joseph Sabine   p. 46
2. Wilfred Owen   p. 57
3. Eldred Bowyer Bower   p. 59
4. Monica Boyce   p. 75
5. Iola McCue   p. 84
6. H. Dennis Bradley   p. 121
7. William Corder   p. 144
8. Barbadian vault   p. 164
9. Sir Stapleton Cotton, later Lord Combermere   p. 169
10. Barbara Mullins   p. 185
11. Peggy Sullivan   p. 188
12. Guy Gibson   p. 190

Introduction

'Life goes, Death never comes.'

from *The Sleeping Beauty* by Edith Sitwell

TO MANY PEOPLE the behaviour of apparitions of the dead, which essentially is the subject of this book, is either so frightening as to hardly bear thinking about, or else is laughed at, albeit somewhat nervously, as an idea produced by a superstitious imagination allied with a nervous disposition, stirred into anxious being by the writers of gothic fiction and their modern descendants.

The latter notion finds its eighteenth-century antithesis in the comforting assurance given by Rasselas, the hero of Samuel Johnson's eponymous novel, to his sister's frightened maid-servant Pekuah. She is portrayed as becoming alarmed when her mistress urges her to enter and explore with their party the inner passages of the Great Pyramid, which she is sure must be haunted by the phantoms of those interred within.

'I will promise you safety,' Rasselas confidently tells her. 'There is no danger from the dead; he that is once buried will be seen no more.'

This suggestion, however, is immediately countered by his travelling companion, the worldly-wise poet Imlac, whose argument for the existence of such spectral figures remains valid today.

'That the dead are seen no more,' said Imlac, 'I will not undertake to maintain, against the concurrent and unvaried testimony of all ages, and of all nations. There is no people, rude or learned, among whom apparitions of the dead are not related

9

and believed. This opinion, which perhaps prevails as far as human nature is diffused, could become universal only by its truth: those that never heard of one another, would not have agreed in a tale which nothing but experience can make credible. That it is doubted by single cavillers, can very little weaken the general evidence; and some who deny it with their tongues confess it by their fears.'

The point Dr Johnson makes strongly through Imlac suggests the veracity of the existence of apparitions of the dead and it finds constant reaffirmation in the testimony of those moderns who have either seen, heard, felt or otherwise experienced such apparitions. Some, of course, may be mistaken by their impressions, for not every cold spot of air felt in a darkened room or the inexplicable creaking heard in the corridor outside, is supernatural in origin, but there are nonetheless sufficient odd occurrences of this type to indicate that we can indeed be contacted by the dead. This is more obvious (and disturbing) when the dead person's ghost or 'soul form' is seen.

Pekuah's fear (which is representative of the alarm felt by many) is not therefore entirely groundless, although, as we shall see, the spirit of a dead person has scant interest in scaring those left behind it, or indeed of remaining long here at all. Rather, the benign deceased loiterers on this Earth (who together make up the vast majority) are typically kept here by their love and affection for, or by their sense of duty towards, the living, whom they may wish to apprise of their continued existence or actually help in some way. The murdered dead, on the other hand, while feeling anguished by the way in which they died, may nevertheless try to bring their killers to justice, if the living fail in this regard.

This book therefore describes the various methods employed by the deceased: firstly to make their presence known to their loved ones left behind them, in order that they can comfort us with a knowledge of their presence; and secondly, by helping us, in the generally modest ways that are permitted to them, to ease our lives by overcoming the everyday frustrations and annoyances to which we are all subject, and aiding us thereby to complete those tasks which we might not otherwise have the energy or patience to do.

It will hopefully also teach you, the reader, how to love, or at least, how to learn to live with, the often unseen entities that sometimes make things go bump in the night.

CHAPTER ONE

Dabbling with Doubles

When she sleeps, her soul, I know,
Goes a wanderer on the air,
Wings where I may never go,
Leaves her lying, still and fair,
Waiting, empty, laid-aside,
Like a dress upon a chair ...

From *Doubts* by Rupert Brooke

THE SPIRITUAL 'soul form' mentioned in the Introduction inhabits the physical body during the latter's life, conforming to its shape and projecting up to about half an inch from its surface, depending on the body part under consideration, to form the surrounding *aura*. The aura, which is transparent, can however often be seen with the naked eye when the background conditions are dark enough to give it prominence. It has a thin outer layer which is darker than the underlying portion, so forming its border and separating it off from the surrounding air. In this regard it resembles the meniscus of water. Some psychics claim to be able to see colours in the aura, whose hue, they say, reflects the mental and physical health of the person.

The early Latin Church father Quintus Tertullian, who joined the heretical Montanist sect in later life, wrote about the frequent visions of a female member of the church:

'Among other things,' says she, 'there was shown to me a soul in bodily form, and it appeared to me like a spirit; but it was no mere something, void of qualities, but rather a thing which could be grasped, soft and translucent and of ethereal colour, in form at all points human.'

The soul form can often, as Rupert Brooke describes above, emerge from its sleeping physical self, when it may independently walk or float around the house or even travel further afield. If it is seen at this time it is invariably reported as looking exactly like the physical person, to the extent that it is frequently mistaken for him or her, although it often appears to be somewhat paler in colour. For this reason it is known as the *double*. The separated double or, to use the German term, *doppelgänger* (meaning 'double-goer') is thus 'an apparition of the living'. Even more remarkably, the double can sometimes separate itself from the physical body when the person is awake, and without the latter being aware of its going. At such moments the person concerned can literally be seen in two places at the same time.

Dennis Bardens, the author of several biographies and two books on the paranormal, once described to me how, when he was on his honeymoon in Cornwall shortly before the Second World War, his double left his sleeping self and was seen by his wife Marie. This surprising and completely unexpected event nicely illustrates the usual nocturnal parting of our two selves.

'My wife and I were in bed together,' related Dennis. 'I was fast asleep and was awakened by my wife, who was clearly terrified. She maintained that she had awakened to see me standing by the bedside looking down on my sleeping figure beside her. I wish I could record that I treated her distress in a sympathetic manner, but she claimed I dismissed the matter with the unhelpful comment, "What are you grumbling about? So you've got two for the price of one"!'

Such a night-time separation of the inner self from the physical self is often prompted by a person falling asleep on his or her back, or turning over on to the back whilst asleep. In such cases, the consciousness, or at least that part which contains the awareness, may accompany the double on its outing (this does not always happen) thereby enabling the double to become cognizant of its surroundings. If this takes place, then when the self-aware double returns to the body and the conjoined twosome wake up, such an 'out-of-body experience' may be recalled as though it had been a dream. However, the sleeping physical body when bereft of its conscious spiritual self cannot rouse itself, or indeed be woken by being shaken, pinched, prodded with needles, or even burned, until that part returns to it.

I recall two occasions when, having fallen asleep in bed on my back, I in due course found myself floating in the air just beneath the ceiling of my bedroom.

The first of these occurrences was the oddest and took place one morning in mid-June, 2000. After having been wakened to greet the day with a cup of tea, I then dozed off again and soon dreamed, or so I thought, that I was standing before the sash window of my bedroom, the bottom half of which, I was surprised to notice, was pushed right up so that it was wide open. Then, to my astonishment, I was suddenly raised or levitated upwards to almost ceiling height, from where I was somehow slowly moved around the room, just beneath the ceiling, to its opposite side. The colour of the ceiling, I noted, appeared to be much whiter and brighter than it actually was. The episode ended when I awoke to find myself still in bed, lying in the same position in which I had fallen asleep. I had evidently been returned to my body, if such a separation had really occurred. The window was now shut.

The second 'dream' experience happened at night, in the early hours of the morning, when I was fast asleep in bed. But then, without knowing how I got there, I suddenly found myself gently floating right underneath my bedroom ceiling, looking at it, while moving about slowly, this way and that, aware of the vertical confining walls when I came to them and the top of the sash window, but without finding an exit for myself anywhere. I was aware of the ceiling's surface, the joins between the adjacent strips of paper, its odd greyish-brown colour (which, it being night, would actually have looked black to the eye), and the various little bumps, depressions, and cracks it bore. My elevated hovering position was to me certainly unusual but not at all alarming. It continued for a little while longer until I woke up to recall what I had evidently been doing.

Lily Stenton, a correspondent from Sheffield, had several similar out-of-body 'astral travel' episodes when she was a teenager. Most happened when she was living at Woodford Bridge in outer London, where she went to work at a garage. The move there, she told me, was 'a very big step for a young girl alone' and the resulting trauma may well have prompted the double separations that she experienced, which began shortly before she left Sheffield. 'On the first occasion,' she revealed, 'I visited a local cinema and then came back to my body.' And they continued during the nine months she remained at Woodford. 'I travelled round the bedroom a lot but I was very afraid and I didn't travel outside again.'

Even more astonishing is the ability of the double to separate itself from the physical body when that part is awake, a parting which may happen spontaneously or be brought about intentionally. Moreover, the conscious centre of awareness may then either stay within the person's brain, so that he or she has no awareness of his or her double's departure, or it may leave with the double, which temporarily becomes its new home. Both alternatives result in the person effectively being in two places at the same time, a phenomenon known as bilocation.

The added stress of some bad nose bleeds, and the anaemia resulting from them, may have helped cause the double separation of the first type that Lily experienced. This took place at the garage about two months after she had started work there, but she knew nothing about it until the following morning, when several customers came in expressing their gladness at seeing her again and their relief that she was all right.

'They said they had seen me the day before in a part of Essex that I wasn't even familiar with and had never been to,' Lily said, very perplexed by what she had been told. 'Apparently I was on a road in the middle of nowhere.'

She was standing beside the road, the customers unanimously

claimed, looking very lost and bewildered, although none of them had been able to stop and render her any assistance because of the difficulty of doing so at that place. And it was only their accounts of her presence at that out-of-the-way spot, some ten miles from the garage, which alerted Lily to the fact that she had been anywhere else but at the garage, where she, or at least her conscious physical self, had been all day.

In this regard it is worthwhile retelling an anecdote about the appearance of a double described to Andrew Lang by a friendly gillie, or sporting helper, whom he engaged while on a fishing holiday in Sutherland. The unusual occurrence, which had happened to the then elderly gillie's father (and was confirmed by him), is included in Lang's *The Book of Dreams and Ghosts*.

'The father had a friend who died in the house which they occupied,' writes Lang. 'The clothes of the deceased hung on pegs in the bedroom. One night the father awoke, and saw a stranger examining and handling the clothes of the defunct. Then came a letter from the dead man's brother, inquiring about the effects. He followed later, and was the stranger seen by my gillie's father.'

Sally Worth, a member of the successful 1940s tap-dance and acrobatic troupe 'The Versatile Monahans', was kind enough to tell me about the visit made by the double of her ex-boyfriend to her bedroom one morning in 1948, which literally changed the course of both their lives. Her experience demonstrates that apparitions of the living can on occasions be just as beneficial to us as can the soul forms or wraiths of the dead.

While playing in a production of the younger Johann Strauss's operetta *A Night in Venice*, which ran for two and a half years in London's West End, Sally had begun dating Peter, the show's electrician. But when she was later introduced to an ex-paratrooper returning from war-time duty, her head was turned and Peter exited her affections. Three years went by, during which time Sally moved back home to Cheam with her parents, while Peter became a half-forgotten part of her past, despite the eventual foundering of her new romance.

'Then I woke up one morning, and – and I could see Peter, who looked very ill,' she revealed. 'It was something very real, as I was fully awake. He was dressed in an off-white shirt and grey trousers, whose colour seemed somehow blurred, and he stood looking up at me from what appeared to be a spiral stairwell of stone steps, but quite narrow, as it was not a big opening. It seemingly ran up to the floor of my bedroom, so I was staring down at him. And he looked so unwell, just awful. I said to myself, "I know he's ill." I had not seen him for three years, and I hadn't been in contact with him at all. Then he and the stairs vanished.'

Sally was so startled and worried by what she had seen, that she resolved to visit Peter's parents and find out for herself what, if anything, was wrong with him, although she was quite certain that something serious must have occurred. But more than that, as she explained, 'the shock of it made me realize that I still had such feelings for him.' Indeed, she burst into tears when she reached his home and Peter's father confirmed that his son had been in a bad way for a long time. The cause of this was explained by Peter's mother, Dorothy, who told her that Peter had developed tuberculosis and that a few days before he had undergone a major operation to arrest the damage to one of his lungs.

'So Peter had appeared to me looking up into my bedroom shortly after the operation, when he was still in intensive care,' she explained. 'Dorothy kindly gave me a photograph of him taken not long before he went into hospital and in it he was dressed in clothes very similar to those I saw him wearing in my vision of that morning.'

But even more remarkable was the fact that the flat in Victoria where Peter had been living with his parents possessed a spiral stone staircase leading down to the basement, just like the one seen by Sally.

The renewal of contact between them encouraged Sally to visit Peter regularly in hospital and also when he returned home. It wasn't long before their rekindled affection for one another grew into love, which in due course rang wedding bells for them and so launched them on a marital voyage that has now lasted for well over fifty years. It was thus a marriage quite wonderfully brought about by Peter's double making an entirely unexpected visit to Sally at home, who certainly had not been thinking about him then, having just woken up.

One late nineteenth-century case describes how a woman who had gone to sleep in her bedroom suddenly found herself downstairs by the front door, wondering how she got there. She could see her surroundings perfectly clearly although it was dark outside, and she was able to ascertain that the front door was securely bolted and that the security chain was in place. She then felt, but without knowing why, that she had to return upstairs quickly.

'She came up noiselessly,' wrote her sister-in-law, 'saw to her relief that the dog had not heard her, looked to the bed ... and saw, to her amazement, her own sleeping body! The sight gave her no sense of alarm, but simply quickened her desire to get back into that body, which with all dispatch she did. This process she can only describe as *dissolving or melting into* her body.'

The woman was quite sure that her experience was not a dream, for during it she felt 'as much awake as in daily life'.

Dennis Bardens, whose new wife saw his double looking down at himself while asleep one night, became the witness to a far more startling double separation when he was recuperating from an operation at the Royal Masonic Hospital, Hammersmith.

'I was sitting alone on a first-floor balcony looking down on to the front entrance and the garden,' he informed me, 'when the main door swung open and a tall, grey-haired man in a patient's red dressing gown came out and walked slowly and deliberately into the sunlit garden. I was astonished to see him followed by the exact duplicate of himself, solid and clearly delineated in the bright sunshine.'

Dennis immediately wondered if the drugs he had been given might be producing the strange duplication, and he looked hurriedly around for a nurse to ascertain if she, too, saw the same, but alas! there wasn't one in the vicinity.

'So I continued to watch intently, having established by moving my eyes around that absolutely nothing else was double. I was too ill at the time to bother to mention it to anyone and it must remain a mystery.'

The tall male patient was evidently not aware of his inner self following along in his footsteps, which had presumably separated itself from him without his knowledge or awareness. Why and how it had done so is inexplicable, but the abandoned physical self nevertheless remained upright and mobile and seemingly unaffected by the strange disassociation.

Even more astonishing is the experience of Nurse M. Hendry of Cleveland, Ohio, who was one day working at a small country hospital in the state helping the surgeon perform an operation. But then, without knowing how it happened and certainly without wishing for it to happen, Nurse Hendry found herself outside her physical body and standing within her double form on the other side of the operating table, looking over the surgeon's shoulder and at her 'real' self standing opposite him. She noted her physical body was still performing her surgical duties without being at all discombobulated by the separation and without being aware that she was being observed by herself from a wholly exterior vantage point!

Such a waking separation of the double, wherein the person's consciousness seems to be centred from his or her physical self is very rare, for usually, as in Lily Stenton's case, it is the double which spontaneously leaves the awake physical body without taking its consciousness with it, or at least without taking that part which is self-aware. For clearly, the physical Nurse Hendry must have retained sufficient nous to react to the surgeon's requests and to otherwise know what she was doing, which suggests that our consciousness can likewise be in two places at the same time, even though our centre of awareness can only be located in one of them.

The nurse was surprised but not at all startled by her new placement and watched the operation and herself with interest until the procedure was completed. At that time she seemed to rise in the air and float over the operating table, alight beside herself, and then merge with ease into her physical body, her consciousness becoming suddenly centred within it as she did so. She was in good health at the time and had never experienced anything like that before or, it seems, since. The surgeon noticed nothing out of the ordinary in her behaviour or in her manner of working while she was thus separated, which therefore did not adversely affect her ability to do her job in any way.

The phenomenon of bilocation makes it possible for people occasionally and bizarrely to see their own double, even though they have no idea, like Lily Stenton, that their inner self has left their body. Such a sighting, however, has an unfortunate reputation as it sometimes foreshadows the beholder's death. This luckily did not happen in the case mentioned below, which happened in 1988 to a ten-year-old London Asian schoolgirl, whom I will identify, at her request, only as S.B.

The girl's school was located in a former eighteenth-century church situated in a deprived area of Hackney, whose toilets, where the incident occurred, were supposed to be haunted, and where, so S.B. told me, 'mysterious sounds like footsteps, scratches, and even screams' had been heard.

'The toilets were very creepy,' she elaborated. 'They were situated in the basement area directly underneath the building. The steps leading down were made of concrete, the floors were concrete, and the lights were quite dim. To actually get to the toilet area, you had to go along a long corridor that was ill-lit.'

On the day in question S.B. needed to excuse herself from class and so make her way downstairs. She was dressed, she recalled, in a royal blue jumper, a white shirt, red corduroy trousers, and pink trainers. She wore her shoulder-length black hair tied back into a pony tail.

There were six cubicles in the toilet area, whose doors had no locks but which would slam back on themselves after they had been opened from the outside to allow someone in. S.B. went into the fourth cubicle.

'I was,' she said, 'totally alone and did not think that I would be caught by another kid while in the toilet.'

However, after doing what she had gone down there to do, S.B. was in the process of pulling up her trousers when she became vaguely aware of some footsteps outside.

'I had nearly finished when the door to my cubicle opened, the light falling on my face as I looked up,' she continued. 'What I saw, was me. It had the same clothes on, the same hairstyle. It was the same height and skin colour, and it was grinning. The only difference to me was its eyes. They were not human because the pupils seemed to be slanting vertically like those of a cat.

'I was so shocked that I blinked and shook my head vigorously. When I opened them, it was gone. But the cubicle door was still thudding shut. There were no more footsteps and all was deathly quiet. I wouldn't say I was scared, but I was very disturbed ... I also knew that I did not want to linger around so I quickly zipped my trousers and ran out of the toilet ... and right up to my classroom, which was two flights of stairs up.'

But despite being made very upset by what had happened, the girl did not tell her teacher about it, although she was asked what was wrong with her. She also made sure that she never went down to the toilets alone again. Being born under the star sign Gemini, she initially explained her experience to herself by supposing that she must somehow have encountered her astrological twin; it was only much later, after watching a TV programme on doppelgängers, that she realized she had actually come face to face with her own double.

The unusual feature of the double's cat-like pupils should not be taken as a negation of the phenomenon. Doubles are rarely as exact as mirror images, and they are never reversed as mirror images are, which of course accounts for some of their oddness when they are seen by their owners. They may be dressed in different clothes, in different colours, have a different hairstyle or hair colour, and show other variations from the 'real' person, including, or so it seems, eyes with odd-shaped pupils.

Even odder is the fact that the double, when seen by the person from whom it emerges, is not always immediately recognizable by him or her. This is partly because, as I mentioned above, the double is not a mirror-image, such as you and I are used to seeing of ourselves in the looking glass, but is instead the right way round. The replication is sometimes made even odder if the double manifests as a younger version of one's physical self, which is gratifyingly confusing to the eye.

This odd state of affairs happened to a friend of mine, whom I shall call Charles Peterson to protect his real identity, who at the time (in the late 1980s) was living in a flat in London's Chelsea near the harbour. Somewhat unnervingly, Charles was shocked to find, on waking one morning in bright daylight, that he was being observed by someone who should not have been there.

'There was this figure sitting on the chair beside my bed looking rather anxiously at me,' he recalled. 'It looked familiar but to this day I can't say who it was. I'm not entirely sure that it didn't resemble me. And I thought to myself, "Who are you?" But there was no sense of menace from it. Then it got up and walked through the (closed) door quite quickly. So I think it might have been my own double or that of my father.'

Charles's uncertainty about the identity of the figure partly arises from the fact that his father died shortly before he was born, so that he has no recollection of him at all.

'The familiarity was of the type that says it's someone whom you've known all your life but can't put a name to,' Charles explained. 'I thought it was sufficiently like me to be me but on the other hand I've never seen my father and he presumably must have looked something like me. My mother, you see, never kept photographs.'

Charles has been fortunate enough to have had several encounters with ghosts in addition to this probable meeting with his double. He says that all have looked completely solid and normal, so that, unless they have worn old-fashioned clothes, they are initially impossible to distinguish from living people until they do something, as did his ostensible double, like walk through a solid door.

In one of my earlier books (*Doubles: The Enigma of the Second Self*) I describe how I managed to separate my consciousness and double together from my supine physical self. This, after many failed attempts, was finally achieved by the complete cessation of thought. Stopping oneself from thinking, however, is very difficult to do, for the mind hates to be left entirely blank and idle, which is not normal to it, and anyway falling asleep so often results from such mental inactivity.

Yet I eventually accomplished the necessary prolonged inner stillness, and, as a consequence, actually left my body. This took place by my inner self being swept through a profound darkness down towards my feet, accompanied by a loud roaring noise. I was startled to note that my double, in which I found myself, felt every bit as enclosing and solid as my supposed 'real' self, which, amazingly enough, became an entity of no importance to me at all. It was just a thing, necessary perhaps until its death, but otherwise entirely inconsequential. This lack of feeling for the material self exactly accords with what many have noticed when they suffered a near-death experience (or NDE), and who likened the body they had left to an old discarded overcoat.

I went no further than the end of my bed, where I was apparently positioned on my hands and knees, facing the other way around, looking towards the far wall and its windows. The room was quite silent. And, having just emerged from darkness and a loud roaring, I stared around me with some bemusement. Further adventure was then effectively prevented by my suddenly noticing my girlfriend (with whom I was staying the night) beside me, kneeling like I was, clad in her nightgown. We looked at one another, our eyes met, and she smiled a secretive smile. Then – bang! I was suddenly returned to my body, which was lying on its back, and thereby roused with a jolt to wakefulness. I looked at my girlfriend. She was lying beside me, gently breathing, fast asleep. I can only explain her smiling presence beside me by assuming that she had somehow been drawn out of herself when I left my body. As she remembered nothing when I later asked her about it, however, her double must have left her sleeping body without her consciousness.

Yet stopping thinking, if persisted in as a non-activity to achieve either double separation or, perchance, union with God, rather surprisingly prompts depression. This is presumably because the mind, when deprived of cerebration but not attaining its desired goal, becomes the victim of dashed hopes. It is so unused to coping with emptiness and disappointment together that it casts a pall of gloom through itself. The Christian mystic St John of the Cross called these intense periods of despondency 'the Dark Night of the Soul'. Indeed, his predecessor Mother Julian, who had a number of mystical visions on Sunday, 8 May 1373, records in her seventh revelation that, after having experienced supreme spiritual pleasure, she began 'to react with a sense of loneliness and depression, and the futility of life: I was so tired of myself that I could scarcely bother to live.' This flip-flopping of her mood was repeated twenty times.

Mental quietude or stillness, which is known as contemplation, is passive in nature, whereas meditation, which involves pondering about and identifying oneself with, say, the Crucifixion of Jesus Christ, is intellectually active. Both methods are age-old ways of attaining divine union, but they do so from, so to speak, different directions. Yet the depression the former so often induces, and which may last for a considerable time, is a formidable barrier to surmount before attaining bliss and knowledge (called nirvana in the East), although nothing that is really worthwhile is gained without one first being tried and tested.

It is therefore not at all surprising to find that darkness, caverns, dragons, ravening wolves, stormy nights and onward struggle feature prominently in those ancient tales of the hero engaged in a quest to attain that which is beyond price, the gold of divinity, for all are symbolic of the black depressive void which must be endured and passed through before either separation or the dizzying heights of divine union can be reached. Edmund Spenser's character Pyrochles in *The Faerie Queene* neatly expresses something of this grim inner wretchedness:

> 'Perdye, then is it fit for me,' (said he)
> 'That am, I weene, most wretched man alive:
> Burning in flames, yet no flames can I see,
> And dying daily, daily yet revive.'

But while the bliss of union may be reached by those who actively seek it, for most of us it is the act of dying that brings us to the gulf beyond and then hurries us across it. Death thus allows the spirit or soul to leave the physical body permanently, while sleep, coma or a NDE can cause only a temporary separation of the two.

When the departure occurs at death (or sometimes just before death), the spirit is traditionally called a *wraith* to distinguish it from the double, an apparition of a living person. The term 'wraith' is typically applied to the newly liberated soul form for several weeks or even months after its body's death, whereupon it becomes a *ghost*, although the two terms are often used interchangeably. In appearance they are, however, essentially identical. In Britain the double was once widely referred to as a *fetch*, and hence 'death-fetch' was more graphically employed to denote the wraith, although different names were also used locally.

It is pertinent to note that the ancient Romans referred to wraiths and ghosts as *manes*, a term believed to derive from the Old Latin root *manis* meaning 'good' or 'propitious'. Hence the plural *manes* is best translated as 'the kindly ones' and accords with the Roman notion that the spirits of the dead not only remain in the vicinity of the house where they had lived and, indeed, where their ashes were kept in cinerary urns, but that they have consciousness and, most importantly, are well disposed towards their still-living family members, whom they try, where possible, to help. The Roman concept of 'the helpful dead' was widely believed in the ancient world, as it still is in many Eastern countries, and is the fundamental proposition behind this book.

Yet before proceeding further with wraiths I would like to mention a remarkable nineteenth-century case of bilocation, which was recorded by J.G. Keulemans, a sitter at the spirit séance in question, which occurred in July 1884 at Barnsbury. It involved the replication of the medium in attendance, and both the man and his double were witnessed by all present due to the simultaneous shining of a helpful, bright 'spirit light'.

'Our medium, Mr Husk, was seated at the table, hands being linked as usual,' said Mr Keulemans. 'Towards the close of the séance – after our familiar "John King" had left the circle – a tremendously powerful light, illuminating the entire room, suddenly appeared over our heads, every one present being visible.

'I saw the double of the medium standing erect and holding this spirit light in his outstretched right hand. Yet at the same moment, I saw the medium seated in his usual place! There was no one present whom I could possibly have mistaken for the figure representing the medium. It was Mr Husk without any doubt, and the person sitting behind this figure was also, undoubtedly, Mr Husk.'

The beneficial light then was moved forwards by the double, although it quickly became much less intense, while remaining bright enough to illuminate 'the partly uncovered forearm' holding it for a short time afterwards, before going out and bringing darkness again to those in the room. Hence nobody unfortunately saw the double return into Mr Husk, and nor evidently did he refer to it doing so.

The double, however, comes into its own as a helper of the living once it has separated itself at death from its constrictive physical self and so gains the freedom of the afterlife.

This will be our subject for the rest of the book.

CHAPTER TWO

Wraiths and Ghosts

He did not die in the night,
He did not die in the day,
But in the morning twilight,
His spirit passed away.

from *A Shameful Death* by William Morris

WHEN IT IS visible, the wraith often replicates the double's paleness and it appears to be as solid as its once-living self. It also often possesses the ability to manipulate matter. This surprising talent was witnessed by a young woman named Elizabeth Hobson, who had had frequent sightings of the spirit forms of dead people. In May 1768 she told John Wesley, the founder of Methodism, who recorded her experiences, that when she had been alone and very ill, the wraith of her deceased uncle and guardian, Thomas Rea, which exactly resembled the once-living man, had frequently visited her during the hours of darkness and was able to bring to her water and/or wine to drink, food to eat, and other like necessities. Yet, despite this capacity, her uncle was seemingly unable to speak to her, in contrast to some of her other nocturnal visitors.

Five years before Wesley's interview with Elizabeth, her brother George Hobson, who was, she notes, 'a good young man', set out on a sea voyage as a member of the ship's crew. The vessel sailed just before the feast of Michaelmas (which falls on 29 September) 1763, which was a Thursday.

'The day after Michaelmas-day, about midnight,' she went on, 'I saw him standing by my bedside, surrounded with a glorious light, and looking earnestly at me. He was wet all over. That night the ship in which he sailed, split upon a rock, and all the crew were drowned.'

She also revealed that on Thursday, 9 April 1767, likewise at about midnight, when she was still awake, she saw her other brother John standing by her bedside. Hence she was not entirely shocked to learn later that 'just at that time he died in Jamaica'.

The wraith, however, is enigmatic in nature, for while it does display quasi-physical capabilities, which sometimes enable it to lift and carry objects, both it and the ghost can, as the following case reveals, pass through doors and even walls like the typical double, while if pursued and cornered, say, in a room they can rapidly fade away to nothingness and so vanish from sight. Both are also able to do the opposite of this and come suddenly into view out of thin air. Moreover, the wraith and ghost can make their presence felt without being seen, and even more intriguingly they may sometimes become visible to one or two people in a group but not to the others. The latter suggests that a degree of psychic sensitivity is necessary before they can be witnessed.

In 1973 the aforementioned Charles Peterson became the tenant of a small farm in Suffolk which included a large, delightful sixteenth-century thatched farmhouse with a moat, latched doors and enormous timbers, in which the bedrooms led one into the other, so that everything was entirely right for the period.

'I'd only been there about a week or so,' Charles recalled, 'and was lying in bed one night reading, when suddenly a movement caught my eye. And from the inner bedroom door I saw a woman dressed in eighteenth-century-style clothes, a farmer's wife or someone, rather plump in build, wearing a linen hat and, over her dress, a long apron, which she was busily adjusting as she walked across from the inner bedroom and out towards the door of my bedroom. She paid no attention to me at all!

'And I was astonished. I gazed dumbfoundedly at this figure as it crossed the double bedroom – and it had some little way to go – and then I saw it just disappear without opening the door on to the landing. It walked through the door, although the figure looked absolutely solid! Whoever it was, it was entirely unmalicious and seems to have been, or so I presumed, a previous inhabitant of the place.'

Hardly surprisingly Charles did not sleep that night.

A similar surprising encounter with a ghost happened to Paul Pearson when he and his wife Sylvia lived in an early nineteenth-century house in St John's, Newfoundland, back in the early 1970s. The couple's dog was the first to sense the presence of otherworldly visitors there. The principal focus of its attention was an old chair which had been left behind by the previous tenants. Almost every day as darkness fell the dog would howl at the chair, which was both strange and disturbing for the couple, and even more mysteriously, if anything was laid on the chair, the item would often disappear, sometimes for a few days, but sometimes for good. In the end, of course, the chair had to go.

But Paul recalled one day with a particular shudder, when he went to relieve himself.

'I found this guy in the bathroom adjusting his tie and combing his hair,' he said. 'He was in his mid-fifties and wore a dark grey suit. I stood at the door stunned. Then he finished what he was doing, turned round, walked right through the bath, through the wall and out. I ran back to tell Sylvia what I'd seen when this wind just blew up and blew open the front double door. One door blew in and the other blew out. We were petrified.'

Not long afterwards the Pearsons moved to Montreal, where they bought a modern house. But this did not lead to their ghostly experiences stopping, as we shall discover in Chapter Six.

More happily, in 1994 a Belgian friend of a married couple I once met was in the process of moving house, and asked them if they would put him up for a few nights because the flat into which he was due to move was not ready for him to take up residence, owing to some uncompleted repairs. The couple, Brian and Anne-Marie, who were then residing in their nineteenth-century *pied-à-terre* in a village just outside Brussels, said that although they were due to go away on holiday he was perfectly welcome to stay and that they would show him his bedroom and leave him a key before they left. They warned him that, because their middle-aged next-door neighbour also had a key and was used to popping in regularly to keep an eye on the place for them, he should not be surprised to see her there now and then.

When Brian and Anne-Marie came back two weeks later, the friend returned the key to them, thanked them for their kindness, and said: 'The old lady's very pleasant, isn't she?'

To which Anne-Marie replied, 'Well, I wouldn't exactly call her an old lady, if you mean our next-door neighbour.'

'No, I didn't mean her,' he replied. 'I mean the old lady who sits beside the fireplace in the lounge. I saw her there most times when I came in. Is she a relative of your neighbour?'

The old woman, however, was completely unknown to Brian and Anne-Marie as she was also to their neighbour, who to her consternation could not think how she had got in.

But then Brian recalled that some months previously he had one day noticed an elderly couple looking at the house with great interest. So he went to ask if he could help them, and the man explained that his grandparents had once owned the property, and that, when he was a small boy, he had often stayed there with them. So Brian invited them in to look around and to see what changes had been made to the place. It was then that the elderly man told him that his grandmother had loved sitting in a chair beside the fireplace, from where she would smile at and talk with him and anyone else who was passing. She had been, he said, a very pleasant and friendly old lady.

Hence it seems that while Brian and Anne-Marie were away the old lady's ghost had appeared to their friend, who had known nothing at all about her, and had been as charming and as welcoming to him when he came home each day as she had once been to friends and family members in her own lifetime.

So how pleasant it was for them to discover that the old lady is evidently still sitting beside the same fireplace and that she will, when a stranger is there all alone, show herself, speak, and make him or her feel right at home.

Like its counterpart the double, the wraith is able to travel to distant places very rapidly, even instantly, which may happen when it wishes to apprise a loved one of its own body's death. The method of contact, moreover, may not be visual at all (although lights are sometimes seen) but effected via the other senses, as touch, hearing, temperature change, etc. These different forms of communication have all been utilized by helpful wraiths.

The departed, however, are sometimes able, or so it seems, to produce a brief surge of energy, which can cross the interface separating us from them and so create a called name, a flash of light, a knock or a sudden touch. It is not usually their intention to cause alarm by doing this, but they are often constrained by what they are able to do when the conditions are somehow right for them to make contact. They are, after all, the denizens of another realm, that of the spirit, where different energies are utilized and different laws apply, which they not only have to get used to and abide by, but which are hard, even impossible, to contravene.

Some wraiths and possibly even some non-human spirits behave mischievously, even maliciously, but these phantoms are fortunately rare. They produce those dramatic and frightening hauntings in which a particular house or family is disturbed by mysterious knocks, raps, furniture movements, footsteps, cold spots, howls, laughter, screams, whispering voices and so on, either singly or concurrently, that are often ascribed to the entity aptly called a *poltergeist*, meaning 'noisy or boisterous ghost'. In modern times, however, such upsetting events are often ascribed to the disruptive psychic forces engendered by an emotionally or sexually disturbed teenage girl, or sometimes boy, but this neat parapsychological explanation is by no means, as we shall see, the only one.

My maternal great-uncle, Walter, who fought in the trenches during the First World War, at one time slept, along with his fellows, in bunks in a covered, protected area, which had a door at the end. At the same time each night the door was abruptly thrown open to crash against the concrete wall alongside it, rousing all the men in their bunks. This was followed by heavy footsteps which came down the passageway between them, but without anyone ever being seen to account for them, which naturally unnerved the soldiers considerably.

The wraith that appears as an apparently solid figure, which it sometimes does shortly after its death, is a very different manifestation from the visitations made by misty shapes or semi-transparent figures, which constitute the archetypal haunting. Such hauntings usually involve ghosts that appear at a similar time of day or night, move in a similar way, follow a similar route, and often originate from those who have died tragically and violently.

The spectre I saw one night around midnight at a Victorian house in Hastings owned by a friend, the late Mrs Diana Speight, and which moved silently past my bed before disappearing through the closed door of the room, certainly had the height and general shape of a person, but it lacked sufficient detail in its opaque, white misty form for its sex to be clearly determined (although I sensed it was a woman), let alone its identity. I only saw it on that one occasion, although it is quite possible that it passed through the room on other nights when I was asleep. And as it brought no noticeable coldness or sense of menace with it, it gave me the impression that it was simply curious about who I was; then, having satisfied itself in that regard, it perhaps felt no further need to intrude itself into the room I was briefly occupying.

That house on St Helen's Road, however, did have one downstairs room whose creepy ambiance led to it being used as a storeroom. It was noticeably colder than other rooms and it was the source from time to time of loud, unaccountable sounds, like bumps, knocks and bangs. More intriguingly, one day a builder, who was working in an adjacent room doing some tiling, looked up from his work and to his great surprise saw, standing in the doorway of that room, a girl who was staring out at him. She was clad in a long black dress with a sort of white frill round her neck, and wore a white cap on her head. At that moment the temperature, the builder said, dropped noticeably, which made him turn and reach for his jacket, but when he looked back at the doorway the strange young woman had vanished. It took him a long time to get properly warm again. The room, moreover, when looked into, was unoccupied.

The intriguingly fully-formed ghost, which was dressed in clothes of a style worn one hundred or more years earlier, and which had stood watching the workman, was presumably curious about what was happening and doubtless wanted to know who was causing the disturbance in the residence that it still occupied!

In the 1930s, my above-mentioned great-uncle Walter and his wife Ada took over the running of the Bell Hotel, a very old pub, in Hemel Hempstead, Hertfordshire. One night they both awoke to see a figure dressed in eighteenth-century clothes standing at the foot of their bed, which naturally alarmed them. (Bed-ends are a favoured spot for both night-visiting wraiths and ghosts to position themselves in.) Walter subsequently investigated the history of the pub to see if anything had occurred there which might account for the visitation. His research turned up the sad fact that one night in the late eighteenth century a man who had gambled away his entire fortune had gone upstairs into what became their bedroom and had there blown his brains out.

Such distinctness of form, however, is not seen by everyone who finds himself or herself in the presence of a ghost.

A striking case in point is the strange experience of Harry Wontner, who visited Versailles with his sister, a Paris resident, in 1926. On reaching the stunning and celebrated Galeries des Glaces, or Hall of Mirrors, which is where, among other historical events, the famous Treaty of Versailles was signed on Sunday, 29 June 1919, Hugh felt compelled to use up the last picture on the roll of film he had in his camera to capture the interior view. He waited until the other sightseers had left the huge room, for his sister had warned him (mistakenly, as it turned out) that the taking of photographs was prohibited there, then positioned himself at one end and snapped a long shot of it. Thereafter the visiting siblings proceeded to enjoy the rest of their tour.

But when Hugh Wontner returned to his residence at Hedsor Priory, Berkshire, and had the film developed, he was very surprised to notice some figures in the print which were certainly not visible in the Hall of Mirrors when he took the photograph.

'It showed,' Hugh wrote to Margaret Gordon Moore, 'the misty outlines of several people, dressed in what appeared to be eighteenth-century clothes, walking in the centre of the room. The figures wore white socks. Above the shoulders of these people there was a gradual fading, and the heads were not visible.'

Hugh Wontner's photograph, in other words, had recorded a group of what can only be described as traditional ghosts, which were not only hazy in form but headless, although this was due to their heads not being properly formed and delineated, rather than them being carried under their arms. The capacity of photographic film to capture the location and shape of ghostly figures is remarkable, particularly as their appearance can often be recorded far more clearly than the faint, wispy outlines seen in Hugh Wonton's picture.

But headless apparitions have been encountered on many occasions and their lack in this regard is comparatively common. They are not particularly pleasant to see, especially when the remainder of the ghost is as solid-looking as an actual person. I have thankfully had only one sighting of such a spectre and I would be more than happy if it was my last.

The startling visitation took place in my own living room about two months before I finished work on this book. It was about 11.30 p.m. and I was sitting in the semi-darkness talking to my two plants before retiring to bed.

Suddenly, I became conscious of a movement in the air off to my immediate left, which I thought was the arrival of my frequently-appearing guardian spirit.

But then, as I turned my head towards it, I clearly saw, in the two or three seconds that it remained visible, the figure of a woman, which had manifested about three feet from the chair. She was standing upright and was wearing a tight-fitting, long-sleeved light-coloured sweater, which had a very noticeable chequered stripe that ran down the outside of her left arm, the nearest to me, from her shoulder to her wrist. The unannounced arrival of this figure gave me a nasty shock, not least because it was completely headless, although its arms and torso and the top of its skirted legs were fully discernible. I was at the same time assailed by a coldness that swept over me from behind, the two together not only raised my heart-beat but had me abrading whatever spirit was responsible for the materialization by saying that I did not appreciate being startled like that.

The unexpected shock to my system that this headless appari-tion gave me put paid to any further communication with the plants. The mystery of its visit was deepened by the fact that no one has died in the flat I now occupy; nor has anybody, to the best of my knowledge, done so in the one below.

Phantoms without faces also sometimes appear, despite the rest of their head and body being present, and looking entirely solid. One ghastly encounter with such a ghost was reported to have happened to a 23-year-old miner named Stephen Dimbleby, when he was about to start his night-shift at the Silverwood colliery, at Rotherham, South Yorkshire, in 1982.

As he walked towards the coal seam, Stephen saw a figure

approach him wearing, he said, 'a waistcoat and a grubby shirt, and he had an old-fashioned square-shaped helmet with a light on it'. The man stopped him in mid-stride. Stephen at first thought it was a colleague who was messing about but, when his helmet light fell on the man's face, he noticed with horror that it had no eyes, nose or mouth. It was just a blank space.

'When I saw he had no face I tried to shout but I was dumb-struck. I just dropped my gear and ran to get out.'

Stephen ran for over a mile before finally reaching a pit deputy, into whose arms he fell, screaming.

Later it transpired that a miner had been killed in the same tunnel fourteen years before. The man had apparently been trapped in a coal-cutting machine, which presumably had removed his face in the awful accident. Stephen Dimbleby, perhaps not surprisingly, was so disturbed by what he saw that he got himself transferred to a surface job.

It is not at all uncommon for a ghost to be seen frequently at a particular spot in a house or garden and sometimes over a long period of time. Such continuance, however, does not always mean that the ghost's former physical life there was unhappy or tragic. Sometimes the opposite is true, so that a place which was once loved and familiar continues to be visited by the ghost of a dead person (*vide* the old lady in the Belgium *pied-à-terre* mentioned previously) because it remains emotionally important to him or her. Part or most of the attraction, of course, may initially have stemmed from a loved one still residing there.

But quite often when a couple is parted by death the remaining spouse or partner moves to another residence, either because the house is too large, or, as sometimes happens, because it was a tied house and the widow has to vacate it for her loved one's replacement. When there is a forced move the heartache and sense of loss is made worse for the living spouse or partner, who will look back at their former home and the life they spent there together with regret and with memories of a vanished idyll. This sense of loss, however, can also prove a powerful impetus for the translocation of the bereaved's double, whenever it becomes free of its body, which often happens, as we have seen, in sleep, encouraging it to revisit scenes of former happiness, especially when these may also provide an opportunity to meet again with the wraith or ghost of the deceased partner.

The explorer John Blashford-Snell, writing in *The Times* in 1998 about a visit he made to the Wiltshire house used as a base by the Scientific Exploration Society, gives an interesting example of such a dual outing of spiritual forms.

Jim and Joan, the wardens of the house at the time, were away on holiday but were due to arrive back the next day. They had left the keys and an explanatory note for Blashford-Snell, and the explorer, having arrived there very late, saw no one within but heard some coughing from the room above, which he assumed came from the couple's teenage son Michael, who had not, or so he understood, gone away with them. So, after downing a glass or two of Scotch from the bottle left for him, he went to bed and slept well.

The following morning Blashford-Snell heard what he took to be the noises made by Michael dressing himself, and then, as he took a bath, the sound of what he presumed were the young man's footsteps descending the stairs. He even saw a shadow fall on the frosted glass of the bathroom door as a figure passed it. Then not long afterwards, as Blashford-Snell dried himself, he heard the footsteps re-ascend the stairs, at which he called out loudly 'Morning, Michael' but rather oddly did not receive an answer.

Not long after the traveller had dressed and had gone down to the kitchen to make himself some breakfast, the two wardens returned from holiday, to whom, after he had warmly greeted them, Blashford-Snell apologized for having woken Michael the night before. He was immediately told by the puzzled parents that Michael was not at home and had not been there for six weeks. So who, they all wondered, was the mysterious person still upstairs? A quick search soon revealed that Michael's bedroom was unoccupied and that the bed had not even been made up. Not only was nobody physically there, but every door and window had been locked to prevent ingress by a stranger.

The couple, however, then divulged to their guest that odd sounds and movements had been heard in the house for quite some time and that an elderly silver-haired lady had more than once been seen in Michael's bedroom, whose sudden vanishing revealed that she was a ghost. More recently a feeling of cold had preceded an even more startling appearance seen by Jim when he was alone in the workshop one day.

'He turned around and there in the open doorway stood a man of medium height, ruddy complexion, 50-ish and dressed like a farmer. He wore an inquisitive smile,' reported the dashing explorer. 'Then he was gone, quite literally into thin air.'

The warden rushed out of the workshop to check if the person concerned was elsewhere in the house, hiding away, but found that there was no one there and that the doors and windows of the empty house were as before all locked. The man therefore had not been physically present.

Intrigued by the mystery, Blashford-Snell made inquiries of the present owner of the farm, a friend of his, who was renting his property to the Scientific Exploration Society at the time. And he eventually learned from him that the silver-haired lady was the ghost of a former tenant of long standing, who had died in the room which became Michael's bedroom, while the ruddy-complexioned man who mysteriously appeared and disappeared that day was once her husband. Her former spouse, however, is not dead and lives ten miles away in another village!

Although the sighting of fully formed apparitions is comparatively rare, their absence is due more to a lack within ourselves than it is to their actual scarcity. They are in fact very plentiful, and may sometimes be so life-like that they are passed by in the street without comment. Elizabeth Hobson told John Wesley about one particular field near her home that was reputed to be haunted, and noted: 'Many persons had been frightened there: and I had myself often seen men and women (so many, at times, that they are out of count) go just by me and vanish away.' Such wandering phantoms, however, are usually beyond our psychic ability to detect, and so go wholly unnoticed.

This is why the experience that the noted Berlin author and bookseller Christoph Friedrich Nicolai (1733–1811) had in early 1791 is so important and relevant, for he was suddenly able to see around him apparitions of both the living and the dead that were seemingly prompted into view by him undergoing, during the course of his work, 'several incidents of a very disagreeable nature' which occurred alongside a vaguely defined 'congestion of the head' from which he had suffered for several years. Christoph Nicolai, to his initial distress and astonishment, saw the first of these unexpected figures on Thursday, 24 February of that year. The ghost was, he realized, that of a deceased male acquaintance, which was, however, quite innocuous in appearance and manner and which never appeared to him again.

'But several other figures showed themselves afterwards very distinctly,' he added, 'sometimes such as I knew, mostly, however, of persons I did not know, and amongst those known to me, were the semblances of both living and deceased persons, but mostly the former; and I made the observation, that acquaintances with whom I daily conversed never appeared to me as phantasms; it was always such as were at a distance.'

As the days passed he saw varying numbers of different people of both sexes, who then, about a month later, began speaking to one another and also to him.

'For the most part they addressed themselves to me,' he explained. 'Those speeches were in general short, and never contained anything disagreeable. Intelligent and respected friends often appeared to me, who endeavoured to console me in my grief, which still left deep traces in my mind. This speaking I heard most frequently when I was alone; though I sometimes heard it in company, intermixed with the conversation of real persons; frequently in single phrases only, but sometimes even in connected discourse.'

'I had become so very familiar with these phantoms,' he later observed, 'that at last they did not excite the least disagreeable emotion, but on the contrary afforded me frequent subjects for amusement and mirth.'

Herr Nicolai not only often saw the figures mingle with his living visitors, who could not, however, see them, but on occasions encountered them riding spectral horses, walking with dogs, or even accompanied by other animals, including birds.

'These figures,' he commented, 'all appeared to me in their natural size, as distinctly as if they had existed in real life, with the several tints on the uncovered parts of the body, and with all the different kinds of colours of clothes. But I think, however, that the colours were somewhat *paler* than they are in nature.

'None of the figures had any distinguishing characteristic; they were neither terrible, ludicrous, nor repulsive; most of them were ordinary in their appearance – some were even agreeable.'

When he tried, by way of experiment, to will the figures of 'several acquaintances' to appear to him he had no success, 'for however accurately I pictured to my mind the figures of such persons, I never once could succeed in my desire of seeing them externally'.

This suggests of course that the persons seen were not a creation of his mind, even though he himself supposed that they were. And, interestingly enough, he never failed to confuse them with living people either, notwithstanding their clarity of form, natural size and colour.

'I knew extremely well,' he divulges, 'when it only appeared to me that the door was opened, and a phantom entered; and when the door really was opened and any person came in.' But then he adds, 'They did not always continue present; they frequently left me altogether, and again appeared for a short or longer space of time, singly or more at once; but, in general, several appeared together.' This naturally suggests that: the figures had an independent, external origin and were apparitions of the living and the dead; that their nature was neither mental nor physical, but spiritual; and that they had their own reasons for being there, which included an evident desire to ameliorate the distress that he was feeling. And in this they were successful because, as Herr Nicolai acknowledges, despite the fact that his 'disorder sensibly increased', meaning I presume his 'congestion of the head', he states that 'I enjoyed a rather good state of health, both in body and mind' during the time he was able to perceive his otherworldly visitors.

When Christoph Nicolai experienced a worsening of his disorder, for which he was taking several medicines, he resolved at last to have leeches applied by a surgeon. This was done on the morning of Wednesday, 20 April, almost two months after the first figure had been seen by him. The procedure sparked great interest among his spiritual visitors, for 'during the operation the room swarmed with human forms of every description, which crowded fast one on another; this continued till half-past four o'clock, exactly the time when the digestion commences'.

The leeches certainly proved efficacious in removing his ability to see the figures any more, as by eight o'clock that evening they had, after losing their colour and speed of movement while remaining clear to see, all vanished directly into the air, leaving him, I would imagine, somewhat bereft. Yet, because he does not state if his 'congestion of the head' also disappeared, it is impossible to say at this late date for what exactly the bleeding by leeches was responsible.

This was an astonishing experience for anyone to have, and it doubtless reveals the sort of benign spiritual attention from both doubles and wraiths that we all receive, and which we all could see, had we sufficient psychic sensitivity to do so. It also reinforces the notion, which the other cases considered in this book reveal, that the souls of the dead retain their interest in the living and will help us and comfort us whenever they can.

A further facet of the incident suggestive of its reality is that Christoph Nicolai did not see the figures when he closed his eyes at night to sleep, although one or more were invariably visible in the room when he opened them in the morning; indeed, he sometimes also saw them when he woke in the night. Their external presence means that he did not have to sally forth in his sleep to make contact with them, or to hear them speak.

CHAPTER THREE

The Departed Make Contact

Year after year, where Andrew came,
Comes evening down the glade,
And still there sits a moonshine ghost
Where sat the sunshine maid.

from *The Ballad of Keith Ravelston,* trad.

IN THE PREVIOUS chapter I discussed some of the ways in which
the wraith or novice ghost can contact those it has left behind
on Earth. We must now examine these remarkable and unexpected forms of communication more fully, as wraiths use a
variety of methods to get their message across or at least to stay
in touch. Indeed, any prolonged delay in their doing so usually
only occurs when they have difficulty in breaching the psychic
divide which separates them from us, and some wraiths are less
adept at this breaching than others.

Contact is further complicated by the fact that we, the living,
vary greatly in our psychic ability, with some entirely lacking
this propensity, while others are downright hostile, like
Rasselas, to the very idea of there being a next world. Most
wraiths find it virtually impossible to get through to such blinkered materialists. But even if a wraith's targeted loved one is
open to such contact, the wraith still has to decide: what
message or action would be most beneficial to him or her;
whether or not it is wise to make contact; and, indeed, if such
assistance is allowed. For no wraith has an entirely free hand in
these matters, but must obey, or so it seems, certain rules of

conduct. Any breaking of the rules, as we shall discover, results in a temporary suspension of the wraith's power to engage with us. The length of this suspension depends on what has been wrongly done or attempted and, at worst, a complete cessation of contact occurs.

The most dramatic and effective method of contact is the 'full-bodied' appearance, like those figures seen by Christoph Nicolai, whereby the wraith manifests looking and behaving just as its physical self did, even to the extent of it sometimes being able to move or lift objects in its vicinity.

The arrival of the fully constituted wraith of Thomas Rea was of this type, and many other returnees have proved to be equally solid and visible. Thomas's purpose was to comfort and give direct assistance to his sick niece, Elizabeth Hobson, whom he had brought up and of whom he was very fond. In this capacity he was entirely successful, for he was able to make several nocturnal visits to her room during her illness. We may also take it as evident that his presence naturally confirmed to her his continued existence after bodily death, and that she need have no fears in this regard for herself. This point was brought dramatically home to her on his last visit, when Elizabeth saw him attired in a long white robe and accompanied by a similarly clad angelic companion. She heard beautiful music playing when they departed together.

About a year later a friend of Elizabeth, a young sailor named John Simpson, was drowned and lost while at sea, and his wraith; also soon appeared to her, dramatically wet with brine, as if to emphasize the nature of his death; a quirky feature which has been noted on many other occasions. In fact I revealed earlier that her brother George had also been drowned at sea and had likewise appeared to her wet all over, yet surrounded by a shining light. At first the visits of John Simpson's wraith happened between eleven and two o'clock at night, but within a week it also turned up during the day, namely at sunrise, noon and sunset. Its coming was announced, to Elizabeth's amazement, by a sweet music, which also sounded when it left her.

The surprising feature of the appearances of John's wraith, apart from their frequency, was the fact that it soon began speaking to Elizabeth, although she initially lacked the courage to respond and engage it in conversation. However, once she had overcome her fears and had broached the subject of the purpose of its visits, the wraith explained that it could not find any rest until she had fulfilled her promise to look after its children. Elizabeth therefore reaffirmed her commitment in that regard. The wraith then advised her not to go to the island of Jamaica to join her brother, or ever to marry, as neither venture would work out well for her.

When Elizabeth expressed a wish to be in the next world herself, she was advised that her time had not yet come, the wraith adding, 'And yet, if you knew as much as I do, you would not care how soon you died.' It also spoke briefly but resolutely about how time was spent in the beyond. 'In songs of praise,' it disclosed. 'But of this you will know more by and by: for where I am, you will surely be.' Then it said somewhat peevishly, 'I have lost much happiness by coming to you. And I should not have stayed so long without using other means to make you speak: but the Lord would not suffer me to fright you.'

The primary purpose of the wraith's visits was therefore, or so it seems, to ease its own anxiety about its children's welfare by ensuring that they received the promised help they deserved and needed. Elizabeth benefited from the useful advice she received, although whether this was a permitted function of the wraith is another matter. She also benefited philosophically, by the wraith itself being a manifestation of the existence of life after death and by her learning from it some information about how time was spent in the beyond.

A delightful, yet poignant, example of a visit by the figure of an entire wraith, which occurred in the late eighteenth century, is worth mentioning here. It happened to a nine-year-old boy living at Maidstone, Kent, whose Christian name was Beal. One night after he had been put into his four-poster curtained bed, he was aroused by the sound of the curtains at one side being drawn back, and he saw his mother standing there in the gap, looking at him with a smile. She then bent down, put out a hand to touch his face gently, and said in a loving way, 'Beal, be a good boy, and fear God.'

The child, of course, was not in the least alarmed by the sight of his mother nor by the touch of her hand. He had no inkling that it was not her ordinary physical self, and he soon comfortably went back to sleep.

The next morning, on recalling his mother's visit and the somewhat unusual injunction he had been given, Beal related his experience to another member of the family. He was then told, amid an outpouring of tears, that his mother had collapsed and died of apoplexy (or a cranial stroke) the previous night, at about the same time that she had apparently visited him, which thus had prevented her from actually coming into his bedroom. As Beal had suffered no previous anxiety about his mother's health, for she had seemed entirely well when he went to bed, it is quite unlikely that either worry or, indeed, expectation could have caused him to conjure up her apparition.

This further illustrates the ability of the wraith to appear as a quasi-physical replica of its physical self, with sufficient solidity to undraw curtains and to render its touch perfectly discernible, and with a consciousness alert enough to know what it was doing and thereby to impart a meaningful message. In fact, his mother's wraith, in the few words it spoke, told Beal all he needed to know to guide him satisfactorily through life.

A little-known occurrence of a similar sort happened to Joseph Sabine (c. 1661–1739), whose family seat was at Tewin, in Hertfordshire. Joseph Sabine was appointed captain of the Ingoldsby Foot in 1689, made colonel of the regiment in 1703, when he served in the Netherlands during the War of the Spanish Succession, and had become its brigadier by the time 'he animated the soldiers by his example' at Oudenarde in 1708. Later that same year he took part in the siege of Lisle, when he received the wounds which are central to the story.

Joseph Sabine saw his dead wife at the foot of his sickbed

At the time Joseph Sabine was married to a woman whom he loved dearly and whose apparition he was surprised to see one night. A biographer records that 'he used to tell his friends, he had seen her apparition. It might have been *dangerous* to have denied the assertion, but it would have been very foolish to have believed it'.

Indeed, the belief in ghosts and fairies, which was prevalent then amongst the common people, came under increasing attack from the intelligentsia as the eighteenth century progressed, culminating in the very denial of God by some of their modern descendants.

On the night in question, as Brigadier Sabine was in the process of recovering from his serious wounds, he lay awake in his curtained bed, in a room where a candle gave some exterior illumination. He was then suddenly surprised to see and hear the curtains at the end of the bed pulled back, to reveal, in the gap produced, the figure of his dear wife, who was back in England. He had hardly time to take in the amazing sight, when

she faded from view and so disappeared. Her coming immediately put him into a deep reflective mood as to the meaning of
her appearance.

The answer came not long afterwards, when Sabine received
the unhappy news that his wife had died at Tewin on the night
he had seen her apparition and at about the same time.

And General Sabine, as he became, and later, indeed, Member
of Parliament for Berwick-upon-Tweed (1727) and also
Governor of Gibraltar (1730), would animadvert upon those
who ridiculed the reality of apparitions by saying, 'I can, from
my own knowledge in this instance, confidently oppose [them]
upon the strongest grounds.'

The ability of a wraith to interact with matter was demonstrated even more dramatically by my wife's deceased brother
Frank, although we unfortunately never met because the motor-
cycle accident in which he died took place some two years
before she and I met. His return to Earth as a visible wraith
happened not long after he had been killed.

Until the night of his accident, Frank had lived at home with
his mother and my wife-to-be, where he had of course his own
bedroom. In the weeks following the fatal smash, when the
shock of his death still hung heavily over the house, his mother
had, on different occasions, invited three or four concerned
female friends and relatives to stay, who were lodged for the
night in Frank's room. None of the women, however, wished to
repeat the experience, as all, much to their distress, were woken
in the night by Frank's wraith, looking just as he had done in life,
except that he was evidently much put out at finding someone
else in his bed. Indeed, his wraith showed its annoyance by
taking hold of the bed-frame and shaking it vigorously to wake
up whoever was there and to get them out of it. He also sometimes pulled the bedclothes off them. Most thereupon fled the
room in stark terror, clutching their nightgowns around them.

Frank's mother, being a practical woman, solved the problem
by sleeping in his bedroom herself when a visitor came and
giving up her own room to the person concerned. Her son did

not object to her being in his bed, and left her unmolested, although his disturbing antics were still extended to anyone else who slept there. This is why when my future mother-in-law vacated the flat, which formed part of a large country house, Frank's old room had to be sealed up and left unused.

The startling return of Frank's wraith, while very upsetting to the disturbed guests, dramatically demonstrated his post-mortem existence to his mother and sister, even though neither witnessed it then. Frank's hostile response to strangers in his room reveals that if death happens suddenly and unexpectedly, as his did, the departed wraith can be left in a state of shock and confusion. This doubtless implies that the wraith will therefore reach the beyond without any awareness of what has happened to it and so is quite unprepared for its arrival there; it will probably also miss out on whatever welcoming party is normally provided to give it advice, guidance and counsel.

Lacking such assistance, it therefore struggles to understand what has happened to it. Very often it then tries to hurry back to the world it knows and to those activities and relationships with which it is familiar, and so resume its interrupted life. It will of course gradually understand, upon returning here, that something is very wrong, for it must suffer a good deal of frustration in trying to communicate with those it knows and loves. However, when living people leave their bodies in their double form during sleep, as many do, they are able to interact with any wraith they encounter as readily as they once all could as their physical selves. And if they can also sometimes manifest together as visible entities, as is certainly possible, then their interaction with the ordinary world of materiality will be temporarily complete.

But, while Frank did not appear to his sister back then, she did see him ten years later, when she and I were married and living in Montreal, Canada. One afternoon there we dropped in on two friends of ours, Harry and Brenda, who lived next door in a small ex-chauffeur's flat above a garage. Another couple, George and Beryl, were there, as was Mike, the third member of the rock band Wizard in which he, Harry and George played.

The living room in which we were gathered was rectangular in shape with a window in one of the longest walls, under which was a sofa. The doorway leading into the room stood across from that piece of furniture. At the time of the incident I was standing to one side of the door talking to George, the guitarist, and my wife was sitting on the sofa with Beryl, while Brenda, Harry and Mike were standing and talking together further down the room. We were all drinking beer or wine, but nobody was inebriated.

Suddenly, I saw my wife look with some astonishment towards the doorway. Her attention then became fixed upon it, as if she had seen something there of great interest, even wonder. Not only did she stop talking but she lost any interest in what the others were saying, her face simultaneously becoming suffused with a lovely glow, and her eyes with a wonderful brightness, so that she became beautiful beyond the ordinary. I naturally followed her gaze towards the doorway, as did the others, one by one, but there was nothing visible there which could explain her change of countenance.

Puzzled, I called out, 'Sweetheart, what is it?'

'It's – it's my brother Frank,' she said, without taking her eyes from the doorway.

I think I must have gaped bemusedly. Her reply was so incredible and so unexpected. As I've just said, I never knew Frank, who had been a keen horse-rider as well as motor-cyclist, but she had often spoken of him.

'Where? What's he doing?' I gulped, nonplussed, looking towards the empty space again.

'He's there, standing in the doorway, just looking at me,' she replied. Her expression became even softer and more glowing as she spoke, indicating her heightened emotion. I had never seen her look so entranced. Yet she must have glanced at me and seen the doubt in my face, as she added emphatically: 'He *is* there!' Her eyes returned to the doorway. I gulped again.

The others looked at each other, taken aback, nobody knowing quite what to say or do. All were startled, some dumbfounded, and Mike, the drummer, sniggered mockingly. I went across to my wife, took her hand, and sat down beside her, turning towards the open door as I did so. But it was just as empty from there, at least it was to me, and nobody else in the room, or so it seemed, could see anything. A mumble of conversation around us began again, breaking the tension. It was not long afterwards that Frank apparently faded away, for when I asked my wife if he was still there, she shook her head sadly, and said, 'No, he's gone now.'

Later questions revealed that Frank had appeared in the doorway looking as she remembered him in his last, twenty-first year of life, wearing the same casual clothes. I have an idea that she said he was clad in a motor-cycle jacket, but I can't be sure about that now. I have often wondered why he chose to pick that afternoon to show himself, and that location, so far from the English county where he had lived and died, and so long afterwards. The presence of three motor-bikes in the garage below us might perhaps have prompted my wife to hallucinate her dead brother, as might be claimed but, as she had seen the machines on several occasions beforehand without being morbidly influenced by them, it makes that explanation unlikely.

The occurrence was baffling to us, the onlookers, but entirely real and very moving to my wife. I have no doubt that she saw what she said she did. Nothing else could explain the flush of recognition she radiated. It was, of course, an amazing experience for her to see her sadly missed brother again, despite the above-mentioned questions of time and place that the apparition raised.

My wife said nothing to Frank's ghost, but that is hardly surprising in view of its sudden, unexpected appearance and the relatively short time that it lasted. And neither did it say anything to her. Yet the purpose of Frank's visit, I now believe, was not to converse but simply to show himself to her, by which act he affirmed his continued existence; he was even as youthful and as recognizably himself as before. His presence also revealed that he was no longer in a quandary about where he was, and that he had come to terms with his new situation. This was all my wife needed to know and it did not concern anyone else in the room.

Frank's appearance illustrates that a ghost may wait many years for the right moment to reveal itself, if it ever decides, or is able, to do this. We can only guess at the difficulties involved or the concerns which affect its decision one way or another.

The oddity of a wraith or ghost appearing to only one among several people was discussed, to mention a single example of those who have grappled with the problem, by Gerald of Wales almost nine hundred years ago.

'Spirits cannot be seen with our physical eyes,' he noted, 'unless they themselves assume corporeal existence.'

He then goes on to ask, 'Given that they had assumed such corporeal substance, and thus made themselves visible, how was it that they could not be seen by other individuals who were assuredly present and were standing near?'

And he then suggests not unreasonably, 'Possibly they could be seen only by some supernatural sort of physical vision, rather like that in the Book of Daniel, when King Belshazzar saw the writing on the wall.'

The next sighting of a ghost which deserves notice was by Brenda Collins, of Poole, Dorset, and her husband in July 2008. The incident took place on a Tuesday afternoon, when Brenda was returning, with her husband John, from a visit to his daughter's house. Brenda had felt uncharacteristically quiet and strangely anxious the day before, yet without knowing why, and was still wondering about her sudden slump in mood. The pair nevertheless decided to walk home along Layton Road, past the house where Brenda's former husband had once lived as a boy with his mother. Her ex had long ago moved away, and his mother had been dead for several years. The property had previously been the residence of her ex-mother-in-law's mother. It was at that point in their walk that Brenda suddenly recalled that her former spouse's brother had died on the same date one year before.

Neither Brenda nor John, however, expected to see anybody they knew in the house's garden, not least because a bush in the next-door neighbour's garden had grown so large that its branches obscured the view. They could not, however, have been more wrong.

'As we were walking down the road I looked towards the house,' said Brenda, 'and to my amazement I saw my mother-in-law walking in the garden. She was a woman you could not mistake anywhere. And I could see her because the garden had changed back to how it was years ago!

'She was walking around just like she did when she knew you were coming to visit. I turned to John and asked him if he could see her. To my relief, he said he could. When I got home I felt so uneasy it was unbelievable. I could not rest or do anything. Something was wrong.'

The couple soon found out the probable reason why they both had seen so startlingly the ghost of Brenda's deceased mother-in-law striding around her unobstructed garden, and why Brenda's mood had been so unsettled. For at six o'clock their telephone rang. The unexpected caller was ringing to give Brenda the sad news that her ex-husband had died two days before, on Sunday, and to offer condolences.

'I was stunned,' said Brenda. 'The next day we walked back down Layton Road to see if they had taken down the big bush which we hadn't seen, but the bush was still there as tall as ever.'

Those who do not believe in life after death will of course try to explain Brenda Collins's sighting of her late mother-in-law as an hallucination engendered by expectation, even though seeing the long-dead woman was the last thing she had expected. The same is true of John, who thus cannot be blamed for inducing either his wife's so-called 'expectation' or her 'hallucination' by telepathy, which is the favoured psychic explanation of how unexplained images are created in other people's minds.

The appearance of a wraith or ghost during the hours of darkness is a well-known phenomenon, and such a sighting is sometimes linked to a previous meeting of both parties at that time of day.

An encounter of this type took place in Maymyo, Burma, between William Hearsey, who was about to depart for India to settle some family business, and his sixteen-year-old son Clarence on New Year's Eve, 1933.

That night William, anxious about his forthcoming journey, went for a stroll on his own, during which excursion he climbed the stairs leading to the servants' quarters at the family's unfinished house, to listen to the music being played for the New Year's Eve Ball taking place at the nearby British Soldiers' Institute. The evening air was cold in the mountain town, and Clarence, becoming worried for his father, set out to look for him, and eventually mounted the same stairs to join him in listening to the Strauss waltzes, until he judged it was too cold for them to be outside any longer. They then went back into the house.

However, in October of that year William Hearsey unfortunately died of fever in faraway Mussoorie, and the following day the sounds of stones hitting the roof and pebbles rattling against the window panes were heard at the by-now completed family home at Maymyo, which were interpreted by Buddhist monks as a sign of William's returning spirit.

Just over two months later on the following New Year's Eve, Clarence took himself off to the cinema, and did not return home until shortly before midnight. As it was another cold night, he walked straight into the kitchen to make a cup of cocoa, when he again heard the sound of Strauss waltzes emerging from the British Soldiers' Institute. They vividly brought back the memory of last New Year's Eve when he had stood with his father listening to them, and he stepped outside to give ear to them again. He soon sensed, however, that he was not alone and, turning towards the steps leading up to the servants' quarters, he saw his father standing at their summit looking down at him, his face bearing the same look of love and concern it had always had for him.

Clarence's reaction was not, however, entirely measured, for he ran back into the house, shouting for his mother and siblings to get up and go and look at father William's ghost. Yet they all, perhaps understandably, refused to do so.

But while the presence of William Hearsey's ghost at the top of a staircase, where it was seen by his son Clarence, can be linked to the pair standing together there the previous year, it so happens that wraiths and ghosts are often seen loitering on staircases, either at their top or at some point below.

Actress Gemma Craven, for example, once divulged in a newspaper interview that she had seen the ghost of her maternal grandfather, who died before she was born, standing in such an elevated position. Strangely enough, she was in the kitchen of her own home at the time.

'One evening my mum and I were in the kitchen having dinner,' she revealed, 'and I looked up and he was standing at the top of the stairs in his army uniform. I said, "Oh look!" My mum looked up and said: "Oh yes, it's your granddad" ... Mum's seen him before, but not at my house!'

A much closer encounter with a wraith happened to Finchley resident, Mary W., in March 1994. Her husband had died on 3 February of that year and Mary was still struggling to come to terms with his loss. Then five weeks later on Wednesday, 9 March, she went to bed relatively early and, having read a few pages of her book and watched some television, lay on her side with her eyes closed, hoping to be soon asleep. The time was 11 p.m. The quiet room was lit by a small nightlight.

But then, quite suddenly, she felt the touch of someone stroking her upper arm, which made her start nervously and flick open her eyes. To her utter astonishment, Mary saw her husband standing beside the bed gazing down at her, looking exactly like he had done before he died. He was even wearing the same red-striped pyjamas that he usually wore for bed, and which, indeed, he had worn on his last day. The shock of seeing him there, however, so frightened Mary, that she jumped out of bed and ran downstairs in a panic, even though her returned spouse had done nothing to alarm her aside from touching her and gazing down lovingly upon her, with a smile on his face.

'When I got downstairs I immediately telephoned my daughter and tremblingly told her what I had just seen,' Mary informed me. 'I felt very shaken. But my daughter calmed me down by insisting that Dad had simply come back to let me know that he still existed as we had known him, and that I should be happy for him and for ourselves. I took her advice and quickly got myself together. Yet, because he never came back to see me, I'm still worried that I scared him off by the way I reacted.'

Yet a visit by an entire wraith, as we have seen, can happen far more quickly after death than this, even though the loved one thus contacted is far away.

A rapid post-mortem visit by a wraith was experienced by one unnamed woman, who was so astonished by the event that she related it to Martyn Pryer, of Westerham in Kent, a former policeman. The pair met when he and the woman and her husband joined, in 1996, a small group in Bexley interested in topics like remote viewing. 'The couple, who were in their sixties,' Martyn told me, 'were well dressed, almost formally so, and unassuming.'

'The lady had a story to tell,' he continued. 'She said that a short while ago she had gone into her living room and had there found the son of a friend of hers sitting in an armchair. He was staring into space and she could get no response from him, so she telephoned his mother. The mother was very taken aback and upset and told the lady that her son had committed suicide the previous day. Shocked, the lady returned to her living room and watched as the young man slowly faded away.'

The incident further brings home the fact that while a wraith can, when it so desires, manifest as a duplicate of its former living physical self, from which it is indistinguishable, it can retreat from it by literally fading away. The dead youth's manifestation to a woman who had no idea he had killed himself implies that she did not create his image from her imagination, although the fact that his mother (and family?) knew of his death does not rule out the possibility of some telepathic leakage from her or them. However, if telepathy is considered as a cause it is difficult to account for the woman generating the youth's image in her own living room, where he had evidently spent no time.

The reason for his wraith's visit to a neighbour is not clear, yet by serving as a buffer between itself and the brutal truth of its body's end, it may have been hoping to save the woman some of the distress that it surely must have witnessed its mother suffering. But this can only be a supposition. The wraiths of young suicides often find themselves in a state of confusion on reaching the other side, where they are not of course supposed to be.

We might, however, compare the lost look of the wraith of the above-mentioned suicide with the far more benign appearance of that of the poet Wilfred Owen, who was shot and killed in France by a German machine-gunner on 4 November 1918. He appeared to his younger brother Harold, who at the time was aboard HMS *Astraea* sailing north from Table Bay, South Africa, over three thousand miles away.

Harold had no knowledge of his sibling's distant death, although he did start to feel increasingly anxious about him from 11 November on. This date not only marked the end of the First World War, but was when Harold's parents received the tragic news about Wilfred. A bout of malaria, however, obliged Harold to remain in his cabin for several days, which deepened his anxiety into severe depression. But, after having recovered sufficiently to take a short walk outside, Harold returned to the cabin to write some letters. On entering it, he saw, to his absolute amazement, his brother Wilfred waiting for him within.

Wilfred Owen appeared to his brother aboard
a distant warship

'I felt shock run through me with appalling force and with it I could feel the blood draining away from my face,' he said. 'I did not sit down but looking at him I spoke quietly: "Wilfred, how did you get here?" He did not rise and I saw that he was involuntarily immobile, but his eyes which had never left mine were alive with the familiar look of trying to make me understand; when I spoke his whole face broke into his sweetest and most endearing dark smile.

'I spoke again. "Wilfred dear, how can you be here? It's just not possible." But still he did not speak but only smiled his most gentle smile ... He was in uniform and I remember thinking how out of place the khaki looked among the cabin furnishings. With this thought I must have turned my eyes away from him; when I looked back the cabin chair was empty.'

The visit by Wilfred's wraith, to a place where the living person could not possibly be, told his brother 'with absolute certainty', as he later remarked, 'that Wilfred was dead'. The visit banished

Harold's depression and, while this low mood was at first naturally replaced with grief and sadness, such painful feelings were
made easier to bear by the fact that Wilfred had demonstrated to
him in the most graphic way possible that he still existed and that
his and Harold's parting was therefore temporary. And, despite
Wilfred's wraith's apparent inability or reluctance to speak, its
presence and warm smile of recognition and greeting showed it to
be fully cognizant of Harold's presence.

A similar long-distance visit by a wraith occurred on 19 March
1917. Early on that Monday morning an English pilot, Captain
Eldred Wolferstone Bowyer Bower, aged twenty-two, who was
flying a RE8 reconnaissance aircraft, was shot down and killed by
German flying ace Lt. Werner Voss, along with Bower's observer
2nd Lieutenant E. Elgey, near St Leger, France. Soon after the
tragedy (taking into account the longitudinal difference in local
times) his married half-sister, Lady Dorothy Spearman, who was
in an hotel bedroom in Calcutta, India, preparing for the chris-
tening later that afternoon of her month-old baby, Alexander
Bowyer, was stunned and amazed to discover Eldred standing
behind her. The shock of seeing him in fact robbed her of the
memory of what she had previously been doing.

'Suddenly I had a very strong feeling that I must turn round,'
Lady Dorothy recalled about the overwhelming event; 'on doing
so I saw my brother, Eldred W. Bowyer Bower. Thinking he was
alive and had been sent out to India, I was simply delighted to
see him and turned round quickly to put the baby in a safe place
on the bed, so that I could go on talking to my brother, then
turned again and put out my hand to him, when I found he was
not there.'

Lady Dorothy's initial reaction to such a sudden disappearance was to think that her brother must have playfully darted
off while she attended to the child and had hidden himself somewhere. But an increasingly frantic search for him by her
eventually ended in anguished realization.

'It was only when I could not find him that I became very
frightened,' she said, 'and the awful fear grew that he might be

Eldred Bowyer Bower manifested to his
half-sister in Calcutta

dead ... Two weeks later I saw in the paper he was missing yet I could not bring myself to believe he had passed away.'

The great distance between France and India was no barrier to Eldred Bowyer Bower's wraith finding its way there or into his sister's temporary bedroom, where he was briefly able to gaze upon both her and his new nephew Alexander. We can only wonder why, having done so, Eldred's wraith was unable to stay longer and so give his sister a better sight of itself.

As to the reason for its visit, we may perhaps suppose that, if Lady Dorothy and her infant son were in Eldred's thoughts at the moment of his death, this may have produced sufficient psychic momentum to direct his wraith into her presence. He would probably not, however, have had time to consider the effect of his wraith's sudden appearance or its subsequent disappearance on her, although its visit would doubtless have eventually been of comfort to her, not least because it demonstrated the continuance of life beyond death.

Just as remarkably, Eldred's wraith that same afternoon also turned up at the house of his married full-sister, Mrs Cicely Chater, who lived in Rangoon, Burma, where it appeared to her three-year-old daughter Elizabeth, or 'Betty', to whom Eldred was affectionately known as 'Uncle Alley Boy' and by whom he was much loved. This naturally suggests that this niece had likewise been in the young aviator's thoughts.

Cicely Chater, who was still in bed, became aware of the strange event when Betty dashed excitedly into her room, shouting with joy that her 'Uncle Alley Boy' had come to visit and telling her mother to hurry down to see him. Cicely immediately tried to disabuse the girl by saying that Eldred could not possibly be there because he was in France, but the child insisted nonetheless that he was. Yet when Mrs Chater went downstairs to check this assertion for herself, she found no sign of Eldred anywhere, much to her and her daughter's disappointment. It was not until a few days later that she learned of Eldred Bower's death on that tragic Monday morning.

During my research into the appearance of Eldred Bowyer Bower's wraith to his half-sister Dorothy in Calcutta and to his niece Elizabeth in Rangoon, I was kindly helped by Dr Tanya Bowyer-Bower. She is a niece of Lady Dorothy, Cicely and Eldred. She confided in me that her mother, Adèle, whose maiden name was Dibble-Chester, had a sighting of her father's wraith shortly after he died. This happened in 1972, when Adèle and daughter Tanya, then aged ten, were living at Ormonde Lodge, Kent Gardens, in Ealing.

For reasons that are unnecessary to expand upon, Adèle had been brought up by an aunt and had therefore seen little of her parents or other siblings; she certainly had had no idea, when the above-mentioned incident occurred, what the state of her father's health was or of his closeness to death. On that morning she woke up and saw, to her astonishment, her father, looking entirely solid and normal, sitting gazing at her from the chair at the end of her bed. She could not understand why he was there or how he could possibly be there. As she grappled with those thoughts and struggled to sit up and speak to him, he simply faded from view and seemingly dissolved into the air.

It was not until later in the morning that Adèle learned that her father had died in the night. He had, as we may suppose, come to pay a last visit to the daughter he had rather neglected in life, and may have been making use of her bed-end chair for quite some time. The question therefore further arises again as to why a wraith so often vanishes from sight as soon as it is seen. This unusual state of affairs is considered more fully below when I describe the remarkable encounter that Charles Peterson had with the nineteenth-century French artist Théodore Géricault, which offers a reason for it.

Yet it is clear that neither Lady Dorothy Spearman nor her niece Betty could have produced a visual hallucination of Eldred Bowyer Bower through their anxious expectation of him being blown out of the sky, for the former was then preoccupied with a far happier event and the latter was far too young to be prey to such fears. And the likelihood of this happening twice so swiftly after the aeronaut's death produces odds running into millions to one against coincidence being a possible cause.

This leaves us with the supposition, which is much favoured by those who dispute the notion that wraiths exist, that Eldred's own thoughts, heightened as they were by the fear provoked by the attack by a German fighter aircraft, were briefly concentrated on his sister Dorothy and on his niece, thereby telepathically creating an hallucinatory image of himself in the visual cortex of their brains. These internally generated images were then respectively 'seen' as an apparent external projection of the figure of himself, much as any incoming visual signal from the retina of the eyes to the brain is similarly projected.

Such an idea will become clearer to the reader if it is acknowledged that what we see around us does not exist as an external reality. We actually create within our own minds the panorama of what is apparently there, based entirely on the extremely narrow portion of the electro-magnetic spectrum to which we are sensitive. But if our retinas contained cells which were sensitive to a wider band of that spectrum, we would be able to detect, like bees and other insects, infra-red and ultra-violet light, for example, or perhaps even X-rays, like Superman. The resulting images would be very different from those we presently create, as would our 'reality'.

But if telepathy had 'transmitted' Eldred's thoughts into the minds of sister Dorothy and niece Betty, it is unlikely that either would 'receive' an external impression of him as they remembered him back in England. For if his thoughts were replete with drama, danger and sheer fear, then they could hardly bring into being the opposite emotions in his loved ones' minds, but would almost certainly produce something of the same ilk in any images generated. And that would be upsetting enough for an adult; it would be overwhelmingly terrifying for a child.

A correspondent in Malvern, Worcestershire, whom I shall call Elizabeth to protect her identity, recently sent me an account of how she once (in 1961) encountered a wraith while outdoors in a busy street, whose appearance was indistinguishable from that of the person whom it was thought to be.

The man, Mr Young, was a well-respected plumber and handyman for one of the two government institutions at Malvern, where Elizabeth's husband also worked. A Welshman by birth, Mr Young possessed distinctive dark-haired Celtic looks, which were emphasized by his predilection for wearing a black donkey jacket and black trousers, a flat hat, a satchel containing his tools slung around his neck, and a love of riding his old bicycle. Elizabeth and her husband had gratefully made use of his expertise on several occasions when, some two years before, they had first moved into their new home, and they had found him capable and conscientious.

Since then, however, all had gone well with the house water supply and the piping system, so the couple had had no further need for Mr Young's plumbing talents. But then, quite suddenly, a problem arose again, and Elizabeth's husband left for work that day intent on locating the Welsh wizard and asking for his help. He returned home, however, annoyed and frustrated by his lack of success, for the needed plumber was unaccountably absent from the institution's workshops or carrying out repairs elsewhere within the perimeter fence.

'Then one day', said Elizabeth, 'I was just coming out of the butcher's when Mr Young passed me by and got on his bike, which was parked at the kerb. I called to him but he didn't take any notice. He just got on his bike and rode away in the direction of his home. I put his not answering down to the traffic being so loud. Then when my husband came in that evening I said I'd encountered him, and my husband said he'd go and book him straight away to do the job.'

Hardly surprisingly, Elizabeth was certain that she had seen the familiar, well-remembered plumber, for his appearance was unmistakable, and she was therefore pleased with herself in the circumstances for having chanced upon him. So she waited nonchalantly for her spouse's return but when he did come back he looked, she said, 'pale and peculiar and he sat down somewhat heavily at the table'.

Elizabeth was surprised beyond measure at her husband's distraught façade and hurriedly asked him what the matter was and whether or not he had managed to catch up with the needed artisan. Her husband swallowed hard before replying.

'I went to his door and rang the bell and his wife answered,' he finally answered in a shaken voice. 'I said to her, could Mr Young come to our house and repair a pipe?

'She said, "My husband died seven months ago."'

When Elizabeth, who was likewise nonplussed by the revelation, had taken it in, she felt sorry for her husband, who was particularly upset at having caused distress to the plumber's wife.

'But I was so happy to have seen Mr Young,' she revealed, 'and I really wish I could have told his wife, only it wasn't the sort of thing to be discussed – not with anyone; it was too valuable for that, also I didn't want to be thought crazy or a liar.'

Elizabeth's remarkable experience of seeing the plumber

seven months after his death left her, she told me, feeling certain 'that somewhere [he] is riding his bike, plying his trade and busying himself with what he does best', nicely concluding, 'and I think that gives us all a clear hope for the future, don't you?'

I agree with her that there is life after death, as the previous cases discussed in this book indicate, although to what extent we pursue our former occupations in the beyond is unclear. We may well have the opportunity of doing so, of course, although I suspect that most people, myself included, would prefer a new challenge in keeping with the new environment. Yet some wraiths, such as those whose physical selves died suddenly, may carry on much as they did in life, at least for a period, and this gives them the opportunity to come fully to terms with where they are and with their altered state of being.

However, I am sure that the deceased Welshman certainly wanted to demonstrate to Elizabeth that he still existed, albeit not in a form capable of carrying out the necessary repairs to her house, but at least in one that was readily recognizable to her, so that, in the minute or so of earthly time available to him, he could show himself to her and thereby indicate his awareness of her need for his services. The sighting of him also put an end to her husband's frustrating search, by directing him to the family doorstep where the truth was to be revealed, and finally by assuring Elizabeth, through a dramatic familiar manifestation, that death is not an end, but a new beginning.

Because wraiths, whose physical bodies have recently died, can manifest as entirely solid-looking simulacra of themselves and thus are virtually indistinguishable from ordinary living people, like the above-mentioned plumber's wraith, it raises the intriguing possibility that some at least of the strangers we encounter in the streets, shops and parks of our neighbourhood may not be as alive as we assume them to be.

In an earlier volume of mine entitled *Supernatural Disappearances* I related how, as a small boy returning from a Devon holiday jaunt to a nearby reservoir, along with a friend, I saw a woman distinctively clad in a polka-dot dress accompanied by a small Yorkshire terrier walking down the narrow country path towards us. Then, when she was about twenty yards away, she suddenly turned to her right and, without hesitation or having to bend, disappeared from view by going through what I assumed must be a sizeable gap in the bordering hedge and so, presumably, into the adjacent pasture field. There was nothing at all odd about that – but what *was* odd was that when we reached the place where she and her dog had vanished there were no gaps at all in the hedge or any sign of her and her pooch in the field.

Equally strange was the fact that my friend had seen neither the woman nor her dog although, because he had been walking behind me, he may not have looked ahead to catch sight of what was to me a perfectly visible oncoming twosome. We did, however, both become very frightened at the idea of such a supernatural disappearance and ran back to our waiting parents, who, having heard my gasped-out tale, laughingly assured me that I was obviously mistaken by what I had seen and that the world, contrary to my boyish impressions, held no occult secrets.

About a year or so after the publication of the book, I was contacted by a sixty-year-old reader from Hull, Yorkshire, named David Lowsley. He had been struck by my above-mentioned experience and had written to describe what had happened to him, which was remarkably similar. It had left him baffled and incredulous, not least because, being a semi-retired biology teacher and researcher, he was used to making observations and to dealing, as he said, 'with facts which can be tested scientifically, and explained logically'. But alas, neither his years of living a normal life nor his scientific training could supply a satisfactory answer to what he had seen happen.

For when visiting a nearby shopping area by foot, it is David's habit first to walk alongside a nearby river, then cut diagonally across some adjacent playing fields to the boundary line of single trees on its far side, and then to go through them into the wide lane leading to the main road. 'It is possible to pass between the trees into the lane,' he explained, 'but there is a large area that has been cleared to allow access for maintenance vehicles.' David is entirely familiar with the locality, and he has walked the same route two or three times every week, rain or shine, 'for a number of years'.

On the October day in question the weather was fine, if somewhat dull, with good visibility. As David Lowsley crossed the playing fields and approached the single row of trees, he suddenly noticed an elderly gentleman accompanied by a small terrier dog, which was off the lead but 'trotting along' close beside him, walking alongside the trees, somewhat ahead of him. David noted that the man was the only other person in the fields then and, when he reached the side of the field behind him, it did not take him long to catch the stranger up.

'He appeared to be in his late seventies, and was walking at a slow pace. I overtook him and as I did so wished him good afternoon. He did not reply,' recounted Mr Lowsley.

'After passing him I walked about ten yards and then turned right to pass through the open gap in the trees. As I did so I glanced to the right – he wasn't there. I assumed he had moved between the trees into the lane but, as I moved through, neither he nor the dog was there. I was surprised and wondered if he had perhaps fallen. I walked back to where I had last seen him but he had vanished. I spent some thirty minutes trying to find where he could have gone, [but] I could find no explanation: he and the dog had just disappeared.'

David Lowsley was so surprised by the event that he returned to the same spot next day and carefully measured the distance and the time it had taken from 'seeing him to not seeing him', which was nine seconds, and he determined that 'there was nowhere I could go in that time which would have put me out of sight of anyone ahead'.

Furthermore, David states that 'I have followed the same route many times but have never [again] seen the man or his dog' and the suddenness of their disappearance has proved so difficult for him to come to terms with that he wishes it had never happened. For, as he says, 'If the man and dog vanished then there is a flaw in the laws of science; if they did not, then no reliance can be placed on what I observe.'

Much more recently another disappearance was noted by him, which in its way is even more astonishing than that involving the elderly man and his dog. Now David enjoys doing research work on creatures called tardigrades, which are tiny arthropods that live in mosses. And one morning in 2007, when he was out walking alongside the river, he unexpectedly came across a fine spread of moss growing all over a concrete slope at the top of its bank, which made a fine sight and which, from a collector's point of view, 'was perfect'.

'But I had nothing to put a sample in and take it home,' David recounted, excited by the find. He therefore went back to his house immediately to find something he could use for that purpose. 'I returned to it within fifteen minutes. There was no moss on the concrete slope or any evidence that there ever had been. Explanation? I am baffled!'

And so, I believe, would anybody else be if they experienced the same thing.

Such incidents are generally scoffed at by those who hear or read of them because they seem so impossible and unbelievable. It is, after all, far easier and more comfortable to assume that the observer is at fault, that he or she did not actually see what he or she claims. And if the charge of 'liar' seems too harsh an accusation, then such unusual happenings are often smiled away by being called tall tales or exaggerations.

Behind this easy assumption lies the often unspoken, yet firmly held notion, which tramps relentlessly through our thoughts, clad in jackboots and arranged in serried ranks, that we live in a rational universe undeviatingly obedient to the so-called laws of nature, from which nothing is free or immune, and which are hurrying us along to some predetermined end, which itself springs, like a frog out of a pond, from the material substrate of its own self.

Yet there is a case for believing that interpenetrating the material and visible realm in which we nominally reside is one that is spiritual and invisible, the two forming a unified whole.

What's more, as I believe, we pass from one to the other at death, our inner spiritual form leaving our physical body and crossing the divide which separates the two. The physical body, meanwhile, decays and is thereby reduced to simpler chemical compounds and so rejoins the earthy landscape from whence we sprang. In life we are conscious of our heavy, cloying physical body; in death, we become free of it, while retaining an awareness of its shape and substance. Hence when wraiths return, as many do, to this world to visit again those whom they love and cherish, they can simulate the properties of physicality to manifest as they were before and interact with others as they once did. Or, if full materialization is denied them, they can speak with an identifiable voice, kiss with identifiable lips, touch with identifiable hands, and sometimes do those things, like healing and informing, which they could not do in life.

The remarkable ability of a wraith to revisit loved ones also extends to places. After all, many people have a favourite outside spot in which they like to loiter, where they find the cares of life can be temporarily forgotten and whose intrinsic quietness, solitude and beauty calms their minds. Such places are often made extra special by the company of a dog, as the joy is shared and thereby enhanced. And dogs are very sensitive both to their surroundings and to their owner's mental state, picking up on his or her inner sense of peace as well as the spiritual underlay that gives places their special appeal.

This leads me to suspect that the reason why David Lowsley and I respectively encountered a person with a dog, both of whom subsequently disappeared, is that we saw a wraith of each walking at a place which was a favourite spot or usual haunt for them during life. Moreover, because the earthly existence of a dog is comparatively short, it typically predeceases its owner by several years, so what could be more natural, when the pair are reunited in death, for him or her to want to take a walk with the beloved pet through scenery which was familiar to them both? After all, the world lying beyond this is by its nature foreign territory, however pleasant it might be, while a remembered walk in the material realm can help ease the two souls back into their former relationship and thereby prepare them for the glorious rambles yet to come in that distant place.

Hence the benefit to David Lowsley and to me, and to anybody else placed in a similar juxtaposition, in glimpsing a unique recapitulation of togetherness in spirit, and thus learning that not only do animals survive death but that so also do the emotions of love, care and concern which develop between humans, dogs and other creatures in life. Furthermore, the realization by us, albeit one we were slow to grasp, that we witnessed a reuniting of wraiths means that those, like ourselves, who are interested in such matters, are not always required to postulate a bending of the laws of the physical world to explain sudden appearances and disappearances.

I examine the fascinating subject of the post-mortem existence of animals and the sighting of their wraiths and ghosts more closely in Chapter Twelve.

Another surprising disappearance occurred in the next case, which furthermore reveals that a wraith can be attracted back here by those material objects that it once created and so had an emotional relationship with, and that such a post-mortem association is maintained for a considerable length of time. The strange happening, which is another of the several encounters with ghosts that Charles Peterson has had, likewise indicates that one of the reasons why comparatively few spectres are seen is because they are prevented from manifesting in our waking presence by the energy field emanating from us.

Charles is an art entrepreneur. He has bought and sold many fine paintings over the years, and in 1989 he had a number of interesting and colourful works decorating the walls of his Chelsea flat. In addition to being psychically sensitive, Charles is also a very light sleeper and is thereby inevitably aroused from his slumbers when he subliminally detects a supernatural presence in his bedroom. Such nocturnal arousals have enabled him to see ghosts that would otherwise have been missed.

'One night I woke up and saw a figure studying one of my

pictures,' he told me. 'His posture was that of an ex-military man, very upright and so on, but a youngish bloke, although he had a strange jacket on because it didn't have epaulettes but patches on the shoulders. And he carried what appeared to be a baton under his arm, which I later realized could have been a painter's brush or even the rod [i.e. maulstick] that a painter uses to steady his hand on.'

The painting which the intruder was closely examining was that of a male nude done by the French military artist Théodore Géricault (1791–1824), who was one of the leading lights of the Romantic Realist movement. Géricault is known to have painted about twenty studies of naked men, of which the whereabouts of half a dozen are known. Hence, that possessed by Charles Peterson may be the only one in Britain. Most of Géricault's other pictures are of horses, sometimes with soldiers riding them, depicted in dashing poses, such as his 'Officer of the Imperial Guard' (1812).

The street lighting which streamed in through Charles's window fell directly on the fascinated spectator of the painting.

'I could see every detail of this very solid or apparently solid figure standing there,' he elaborated, 'and I saw that he looked not unlike the artist himself. Then he crossed the room to go to look at another picture on the opposite wall, and as he was doing that he seemed to become aware of my presence – that I was awake and watching him – because he suddenly turned and looked straight at me and seemed to brace himself in a strange sort of way, as though he felt some sort of energy force or something. Then he was actually pushed back and disappeared right in front of my eyes.'

Charles speculates that the act of waking somehow strengthens whatever energy force we normally have, which is either lacking or reduced when we are asleep, thereby enabling ghosts like the ostensible Théodore Géricault to move around as visible replicas of themselves. If so, this would certainly explain the apparent paucity of ghosts during the daytime and why apparitions of the dead have always been associated with the night.

'But as he became conscious of me because of that energy

field, then he braced himself,' noted Charles wonderingly. 'It was as if he was facing a G-force or something.'

If the apparition was that of Géricault himself, it naturally suggests that the interest an artist has in his or her work in life is maintained for a considerable length of time after his or her death. This is perhaps also true of an art lover.

Charles first became aware of his psychic ability in the early 1960s. This personal discovery happened not long after he had bought a large six-foot by five-and-a-half-foot abstract painting executed by a former miner's son, which seems to have served as the necessary spur for its expression. The painting was hanging on a wall of Charles's West London mews house at the time, following his purchase of it from the artist, who had returned to Devon to teach art.

'I was lying in bed in the early morning and thinking about nothing in particular,' he recalls, 'when what appeared to be a group of miners stepped out of that picture! They walked out one behind the other as if they were traversing a tunnel. They still had their helmets on with the lamps shining as though they were in a tunnel and stepping out of it. It was astonishing to see, although as soon as I became conscious of what was going on it ceased and they all vanished.'

Charles is not of course claiming that the solid-looking figures were ghosts which had somehow been contained within the picture, but rather he thinks that the picture served as a psychic focus from which they emerged, thereby enabling them to be perceived again as a working party of miners, of whom one may well have been its creator's father. Such a notion amplifies what was earlier said about the wraith of Mr Young, who was seen seven months after his death still dressed as a handyman-cum-plumber: that 'life' may continue in this world for many wraiths very much as it formerly did, even where work is concerned, at least for a while. There may be an element of choice in the matter, however, for not everybody will want to keep slogging away at their old job, although for some it may prove a helpful way of introducing them to the next world.

CHAPTER FOUR

Unseen Impressions

She sleeps below,
She wakes and laughs above;
Today, as she walked, let us walk in love:
Tomorrow follow so.

from *My Friend* by Christina Rossetti

ALTHOUGH A DECEASED person may apparently want to appear to a loved one as a fully formed simulacrum of his or her former self, this cannot always be accomplished. Earlier I made mention of the odd fact that sometimes an apparition's head may be missing. The editor William Hone once even had the extraordinary experience of seeing, whilst walking down Fleet Street to consult a medical friend, 'a pair of legs devoid of body, which he was persuaded were his own legs, though not at all like them', keeping pace with him on the opposite side of the roadway. Hone may have been encouraged to suppose that the limbs were somehow the duplicates of his own by the fact that several days later he unmistakably saw his entire double striding along at the same place. Yet judged on their appearance alone the perambulating legs belonged to someone else. They may, of course, have been those of a dead relative or friend, who was worried about him but who was either unable to wholly materialize or who did not wish to disclose his or her identity.

Far more often a visiting wraith is not seen at all but is strongly suspected of being there by the person so contacted. On other occasions it manifests as a spoken voice, a touching hand, a particular sound, or announces its presence by some other means. Several of these contact types are considered in this and subsequent chapters. But sometimes the means of contact can be so unexpected that it leads to the recipient wondering about what has happened.

For example, when my aunt Peggy Sullivan returned home one Thursday in July 1999 after a fortnight spent in hospital, she suddenly found herself thinking that evening about my late wife and what a lovely person she had been. On the following day I telephoned Peggy to congratulate her on being back home, and among the various things we discussed was the dog which belonged to my then-girlfriend, which was a very nice animal.

The next afternoon, which was Saturday, Peggy and her partner Nigel were sitting quietly in their lounge, when there was a sudden loud crash as a photograph of me and my wife and our dog, which stood in a frame on the shelf along with fourteen other photographs, 'just leaped off the shelf' and tumbled noisily down on to the floor. This occurred despite the fact that there had been no movement or vibration anywhere near it and that none of the other framed photographs had moved.

However, although the frame did fall to pieces when it hit the floor, the glass did not break, so it was a simple matter for Nigel to reassemble the picture. Peggy thought the incident 'really spooky' and was sure that it was my wife's way of saying to her 'Thanks for remembering and thinking about me, Peggy'. Peggy also noted that Nigel had no explanation for why the photograph could have so suddenly jumped off the shelf, which indicates that it perhaps moved for the reason she suggested.

Such occurrences are easy enough for the sceptic to dismiss as coincidental happenings, which arise from the chance concurrence of two unrelated events and which therefore have no meaning. But, as we have already noted, the departed do survive beyond the death of their physical bodies, yet have limited powers to interact with us directly, which means that sometimes they are obliged to create some havoc in order to get their point across. And what could be more direct than tipping a photograph frame containing a photograph of yourself, your husband and your dog on to the floor to attract attention to your presence and express a sentiment? Even bright, living people would be hard put to come up with a better ploy in the circumstances.

East Finchley resident Monica Boyce had a childhood replete with sparkle and thrills as a member of Terry's Stage School, where she mastered tap and acrobatic dancing. Her demanding apprenticeship led to chorus-line work and then to a role, along with the aforementioned Sally Worth (see page 16), in a war-time revival of Strauss's operetta *A Night in Venice*, which had a very long hit-run at the Cambridge Theatre in London's West End.

When the show ended Monica joined up with Sally and two other ex-Terry's 'Juveniles' to form 'The Versatile Monahans' touring troupe, who perfected a difficult tumbling technique called 'The Treble Conjunction'. The addition of a male vocalist led to the singing, dancing and acrobatic quintet wowing audiences in variety shows and musical theatres the length and breadth of Britain. But, despite becoming used to the high drama and excitement of those thespian years, Monica was more than a little surprised by the meeting she had many years afterwards with the invisible ghost of her deceased grandmother.

The incident happened in 1999 when Monica was walking along the paved footpath leading from her own home to that of her mother, who lived about one mile away.

'I'd got as far as the Constitution Club, and I had no thought in my mind about my grandmother or anybody like that. I was just thinking normal thoughts,' Monica recollected to me. 'But suddenly I just became aware that I had this very strong feeling that my grandmother was walking next to me. I almost felt I could touch her, although I didn't actually see her.'

Monica Boyce titillated the neighbours with
her garden acrobatics

'I was so sure she was there that I actually spoke to her. She didn't say anything but I could just feel her presence completely. She stayed with me right until we got to my mother's house and, although she couldn't answer back, we had a nice conversation. I reminded her of things that had happened in the past, saying "Do you remember this, Grandma?" Then I would walk in silence, and I felt she was saying to me, "Yes, I remember all those things".'

Monica was, of course, taken aback by this sudden and very noticeable contact by her grandmother, because it had never happened to her before. Nor has it occurred since, despite Monica hoping that it would. Just as remarkable is the fact that her grandmother had died fifteen years earlier, during which period Monica had walked along the same footpath many times to visit her mother, so it seems unlikely that something on the well-used route that day had sparked an intense memory of her deceased relative which she mistook for her unseen presence.

'I felt she'd just come to say, "Hello, I'm still around",' said

Monica gratefully. 'We probably spoke to one another for about twenty-five minutes. It was a wonderful experience for me and I hope it was for her, too.'

Such an encounter with an invisible ghost that remains a silent presence is by no means uncommon, although most contacts of this kind probably take place indoors. The identity of the silent invisible presence is psychically sensed.

Although the recipient of the ghost's attention rarely divines the reason for its sudden arrival, this can sometimes be prompted by tragedy. For example, as Mrs Moore reveals, when a wartime WREN, the fiancée of a young pilot, was travelling aboard the train which was taking her to her new posting, close to her beloved's aerodrome, she suddenly felt that he was sitting next to her. 'It was so real,' she said, 'I had to tell myself I was imagining it because I was so happy, only, strangely, he was trying to comfort me.' Indeed, on reaching her destination the poor girl learned that her fiancé had been killed in a flying accident one hour before. The shock and distress almost killed her.

It is likewise difficult to know why a ghost like that of Monica Boyce's grandmother may wait for such a long time before making contact, except to suggest that the moment and the place have to be just right before it can. In Monica's case, the long hiatus probably didn't mean that her grandmother had found better things to do in the meantime than visit her. Indeed, we can be quite sure that her grandmother, like other wraiths and ghosts, remains interested in her progress through life and keeps a watchful eye on her. The bonds of love, care and concern, as I have pointed out, continue beyond death, and almost all those who 'pass over' try not only to stay in contact with, but to help when they can, loved ones who have been left behind. Yet, as we shall see, there is only so much that they can do and, more importantly, are allowed to do. Wraiths and ghosts also have trouble penetrating, by tactile, vocal or other means accessible to our senses, the interface between them and us, especially when their reaching out is made even more difficult by our scorn, disbelief and blinkered arrogance.

Monica's husband William said his last goodbye to her at a north London hospice just over three years ago. A few days before that happened, while sitting at his bedside, she told him she intended spending a lot of time walking around their flat talking to him when he had gone, to which he replied, 'I'm very, very glad you said that.'

But as it happened, Monica had the chance of moving into sheltered accommodation a few weeks after he died, which opportunity she took, although perhaps hardly surprisingly this did not hinder her husband from locating her or from helping her.

'As soon as I moved in I felt that he was also here,' she told me, 'that he was in the flat.'

Now, throughout her life Monica has had trouble in finding the whereabouts of items she has put down, a propensity which has worsened with age. Her husband, by contrast, always seemed to know where those needed things were, which meant she had come to depend on him for their retrieval.

'He always could find anything,' she explained, 'whereas I would go and search a place perhaps five or six times and rummage about in there and never find what I was looking for. I'm terrible, I'm always losing things.'

It was therefore not long before the newly widowed Monica, who is still stymied by her chronic inability to find missing objects, began appealing to her departed husband for assistance.

'I would say and still do, "Please help me find my glasses, William," or my purse or whatever. "I've got to go out and I must have them with me. If you just point me towards where they'll be, I'll start searching there." Then suddenly it comes into my mind where to look, and invariably I always find what I need, just as he used to find things for me when he was alive. It's amazing really; it's happened lots of times. I get a sense of where it is as though he's putting the thought into my head. I just know he does it. It's never missed. And I have spoken to other widows here and they're all doing the same thing. It isn't just me.'

And to doubters who might try to explain Monica's

mysterious locating impressions by claiming that they really come from her subconscious memory, she gives the example of the much-valued missing ring of hers which had fallen from a shelf and whose bounced and rolled whereabouts she was entirely ignorant.

'I kept saying "I wish I could find that ring",' she explained. 'Then William directed me to the place where it was, which was somewhere where I would never have expected it to be!'

Helping the living to find lost objects is a most useful task for an unseen presence to do and is one that the departed can accomplish without apparently transgressing the rules of behaviour laid down for them. Sometimes, however, someone may call upon a deceased spouse or other close relative for much greater assistance, which remarkably is often given. Jill Eaton of Wells, Somerset, was kind enough to relate to me the way in which her late husband came through for her when she really needed his help.

Jill had sadly lost her husband Alf in the early hours of Boxing Day, 1998, although his passing was entirely peaceful for he died in his sleep, which is perhaps the end that all of us would wish for ourselves.

Like many couples Jill and Alf had discussed life after death and were generally agreed upon its reality, but without having made a post-mortem pact as such. And there was no contact by him of which Jill was aware during the first three months of 1999. But in April of that year things changed, the first change being the arrival of a smell which was very redolent of him (and about which I shall recount more in the next chapter).

However, later that same month Jill spent a day moving a bedroom suite from one room to another. It was a wearying job, with which she resolutely continued until, tired and aching, she was left with shifting the most awkward and heaviest item, her husband's wardrobe. But getting that out of the room proved too difficult for her, mainly because the bulky piece of furniture had become lodged in the doorway. Jill was by then nearly worn out with the strain and effort of it all.

'The wardrobe, half in and half out of the doorway, got two of its legs jammed on a carpet joiner bar and I couldn't shift the thing from where it was stuck,' she told me. 'Frustrated and near collapse with exhaustion, I called out "Alf, help me with this for goodness sake – you moved it a number of times when we were at our old place. So please, help me now."

'With one last gasp, I took control of myself and *pushed* – I didn't have the strength to part lift it and, wonder of wonders, the thing seemed to float straight out of the rut and glided into the room across the floor, ending up in the position where I wanted it.'

Jill is convinced that she did not move the wardrobe by herself to its final resting place, for by that stage the task was simply too much for her. Rather, she believes that her husband Alf heard her plea and used what powers he had acquired in the next world to help her complete the job. For the departed, as we have seen, are always ready to be of assistance if we request it and if what is asked is in their remit to do. I shall examine many other examples of such supernatural aid later on.

But, unfortunately, it is usual for those who have never sensed a silent invisible presence to ascribe its apparent apprehension in others to 'imagination' or to claim that those so assisted simply 'wanted it to happen'. How rich it is for the psychically deprived or neglected to impute so readily an overactive imagination or self-delusion to the recipients of such contacts. Such impertinence is almost as great as that of those who cry 'Where's the scientific proof for it?' whenever someone claims to have seen a wraith or a ghost, but who choose to ignore the fact that a plenitude of observation by ordinary people, as Dr Johnson so justly pointed out, is still scientifically valid, notwithstanding the failure of boffins to sense or see anything themselves. We must also remember that not only are wraiths and ghosts as intelligent as we living (from whom they spring) are but they also have powers beyond our own: hence they are quite capable of outmanoeuvring the average scientist, and probably, indeed, rather enjoy doing so.

Nevertheless, the silent invisible presence has gained an unfortunate reputation over the years because, being unseen and yet capable of affecting our surroundings, it epitomizes the most scary form of a haunting. Yet only a small number of wraiths or ghosts, I believe, ever try to frighten people; most want to help us. The ones that behave badly are spirits which, when in their physical bodies, led unhappy, wretched or murderous lives, and which sometimes had ghastly deaths.

When such unfortunates die they take their unhappiness and trauma with them, and are often unheeding of the healing help which is available to them in the next world. This happens either because they don't want to leave this world or because they feel unready to leave it. Each type therefore becomes the troublesome spirit that hovers in the air of its former home, or at the place where it died, waiting for any visitors, whom it may chill with its coldness or touch with its invisible hand, or unac-countably move objects from one place to another. Later it may behave like a child having a tantrum, and bang doors and windows, stamp along empty corridors, and even rattle bedsteads stacked in an attic. Such a ghost is by then, of course, no longer a silent presence. A scant few can cause actual terror, but they are nonetheless more to be pitied than censured. I shall speak further about their disruptive activities later.

Yet the invisible presence which is perceived in some sensory way is less likely to be explained away as imagination or as self-delusion, particularly if the sound, odour or touch is experienced more than once and by more than one person.

CHAPTER FIVE

Odours and Faces

In the present state of knowledge
It appears wise to believe
As if
The indefinite survival of awareness
Were a feature of reality's pattern.

from *Assumption* by Bradford Shank

THE PERCEPTION OF a characteristic odour connected with a deceased person has been intermittently reported by the bereaved, whose sudden apprehension of it is sufficiently unusual for them to regard the smell as a way by which the departed is letting them know that he or she is still around. By this I do not mean those odours which have impregnated the surroundings occupied by the living person and which, like the strong peluke tobacco smoked by Aleister Crowley, continue to drift into the air of the room for a considerable period after his or her death. More generally there have also been, as Renée Haynes herself has said, 'well-authenticated reports about houses haunted by the scent of pipe-smoke or, more agreeably, by that of bacon frying'. Yet while this is true, I shall here refer to those olfactory impressions which are sometimes smelled in the immediate aftermath of a death or, as may happen, after a longer passage of time, and which, upon being noticed, and often with astonishment, may persist for a few hours or days before finally vanishing, to be smelled no more.

Jill Eaton of Wells, to whom I referred in the last chapter, had such an experience about three months after her husband died, during which period the scent she particularly associated with him had not been at all in evidence, for he was no longer there to use the lotion in question.

'I don't think I could quite describe what I smelt as an odour,' she told me. 'It was more the very peppery scent of carnations. I sensed this around the bungalow two or three times during April of that year [1999]. I detected it immediately. It was the smell of my husband's hair dressing – Morgan's Hair Balm, which he had used since long before I knew him. I believed then, and I still do, that it was his way of telling me that he was still around.'

The distinctive smell was the first clearly recognizable contact that Mrs Eaton had from her husband, but it was by no means the last. I have already mentioned the very useful direct assistance he soon afterwards gave her in moving a heavy wardrobe from one room to another. The three-month hiatus following his death was the time it presumably took him to get used to his new otherworldly environment and to rest and recuperate there before returning here to help his spouse.

Shortly before the onset of the Second World War, London's Camden Town resident Iola McCue's father Neil, a police superintendent in Burma, died of fever while investigating a murder at Marang. When his body was returned to the family home at Victoria Point, Burma, a strong, pleasant perfume was immediately noticed in the air, not only by grieving family members and servants but by those fellow officers who spent the night beside the corpse. This was particularly remarkable because, as Iola's Anglo-Burmese mother May recalled, 'There were no flowers in the compound, or anywhere else for that matter, but there was no denying the unnatural perfume that filled the atmosphere.'

The locals regarded the scent as being Neil McCue's returned spirit, and this supposition gains credence when it is learned that May, while she and Neil were once discussing the possibility of there being an afterlife, had asked him, 'When you pass away, if you go before me, will you give me a sign', to which Neil had laughingly replied, 'Well, all right.' May also made the same promise to him. Thus they had, as many couples have done over the years, made a post-mortem pact, and the floral smell surely was the sign that May had so long before requested.

Iola herself had a similar olfactory experience when May died, albeit many thousands of miles away, and many years later, in England. The striking odour first became noticeable when she and her siblings sat around May's hospital bed, as death came to her, in October 1984.

'I assumed that the other members of my family were also getting the same smell,' Iola told me, 'but when I asked them they were quite puzzled and said, "No". But the smell to me was really quite powerful, and what I could smell was a kind of vegetation. It smelt of sage and thyme, stuff like that, greenery or foliage. And even though it seemed like greenery that was going slightly off, it wasn't unpleasant by any means.'

Iola was aware that the smell was still with her when she walked home from the hospital, and it remained noticeable for the next few days, both when she was at home and when she went out going to supermarkets and shops, but not, she admitted with some relief, when she was eating. And, despite it being present at the same time that the image of her mother on a church wall was visible, as described below, she was neverthe-less, 'totally puzzled and perplexed by it'.

Iola's anxieties about the continuing odour were such that she went to see her doctor about its cause, but he could find nothing physically wrong with her which might explain it. He did suggest, however, that the stress of her mother's death had brought it on, but she did not find the idea very satisfactory.

She later realized, however, that her period of deepest grief was when she was getting the smell, and that not long after it had vanished she stopped thinking about her mother altogether. 'I never again shed a tear for her, nothing like that. My grief had all gone.'

This is why Iola now feels that the strange smell was of great benefit to her, noting that 'when my brother died there was no smell, and it took me much longer to recover from his death.

*Iola McCue saw her mother's face appear
on a church wall*

'Experiencing the smell gave me a feeling of continuity, of a connection between my father's death and my mother's death,' she concluded. 'It was as if my mother was saying, "Accept it, come to terms with it. We don't go on for ever: we're born, we live, we die. Get used to it." '

But the other, even more startling surprise that happened to Iola occurred the day after her mother died when, on looking out of the window of her flat at the church standing on the other side of the road, she saw to her astonishment the impression of her mother's face, clearly delineated, on the wall facing her.

'I noticed it that very first morning,' she explained, 'and I could only see it in daylight, not at night. I could also see it if I went outside the house. I could see the face, the eyes; the features were there, blown up. I saw the head, too, but I can't recall the hair. I didn't see the neck either.'

The image appeared in the middle of the wall and was about six or seven feet in height, with a corresponding breadth, and was turned towards her, as if gazing at her. The features were those of her mother as she had appeared not long before she died, naturally coloured and with a peaceful expression.

The sight was certainly dramatic and unusual, and it persisted, like the odour, for just over a week, although Iola found that having to cope with both strange events and the grief of her mother's loss meant that for her, 'I got to the point where I didn't want to look at it and avoided looking at it.' And yet the image, while eidetic in its clarity, did not appear on any other wall, whether indoors or outdoors, so it could not, for this reason, be regarded as imaginary. Indeed, Iola had never expected to see, nor for that matter had thought of seeing, her mother's physiognomy so brazenly displayed. And, while it is tempting to suppose that her mother might have been using the church in this way to show her that Christianity is the true religion, Iola deprecatingly observed: 'I thought it was an obvious place for it to appear; it was a suitable backdrop.'

A much earlier and less overpowering example of this remarkable phenomenon, quoted by Sir W.F. Barrett, happened six weeks after the death at home of an Australian sea captain named Towns, who died in 1873. The image of the captain appeared within his house near Sydney, New South Wales. It was first noticed by his married daughter, Mrs Lett, and a young female friend, when they went together into one of the other bedrooms. The room was illuminated by gas lamps, which gave sufficient light to render visible the astonishing sight.

'They were amazed to see, reflected as it were on the polished surface of the wardrobe, the image of Captain Towns,' wrote his son-in-law Charles Lett. 'It was barely half-figure, the head, shoulders, and part of the arms only showing – in fact, it was like an ordinary medallion portrait, but life-size. The face appeared wan and pale, as it did before his death, and he wore a kind of grey flannel jacket, in which he had been accustomed to sleep.'

The women at first thought the figure must be the reflection of a picture of Captain Towns but, when they found that there was no such portrait hanging on any of the room's walls, their shrill cries of astonishment quickly brought other members of the household into the bedroom, all of whom, without any prompting, immediately recognized the physiognomy on the wardrobe panel as that of the dead captain.

The image of Captain Towns was thereafter seen in turn by Miss Towns (his other daughter), by his butler, by his nurse, by his elderly valet, by a housemaid, and finally by his widow, making a total of eight adult persons who witnessed it *in situ*. The widow, upon seeing the likeness, passed a loving, yet trembling hand over it, at whose touch it faded from sight and soon disappeared. The mysterious and striking pictorial representation of the old sea dog then never came back.

It is of course impossible to say how May McCue and Captain Towns, resident in the beyond as they then were, managed to pull off such a pictorial coup and so wonderfully to serve notice of their continuing existence to family members and others. The image of Captain Towns gains credence from having been seen by several people, and that observed by Iola is reinforced by the odour of greenery accompanying it, which increases its spiritual import. Neither sighting can reasonably be dismissed as imagination, expectation, or an attack of 'the heebie-jeebies'. Both stand on their own merits as genuine visual contacts from the other world.

Helen Creighton, a Canadian researcher, likewise writes of a Mahone Bay, Nova Scotia, woman who had died of tuberculosis not long after she moved into the house she had always dreamed about, but was nonetheless very happy there for the short period that she remained alive. The carer who looked after the woman in her final illness stayed on at the house, where she had the following similar recurrent experience.

'She told that every once in a while the face of her former patient would appear against the wall,' writes Dr Creighton. 'No more of her was seen, and nothing happened, just the face.'

Even more startling was the sighting that Mrs Florence Margaret Bowyer Bower, the second wife of Thomas Arthur Bowyer Bower and mother of Cicely and Eldred, had of her dead son's face one night when she was in bed, for its physiognomy did not appear as a complete likeness but gradually came into being, feature by feature, in the darkness.

As I have already described, the entire wraith of Eldred W. Bowyer Bower, who was shot down and killed in France on 19 March 1917, briefly appeared to his half-sister in India and to a niece in Burma that same morning. Yet neither his mother nor his fiancée were so distinguished in the immediate aftermath of his death, which at first seems somewhat thoughtless, if not callous, of Eldred's wraith in the circumstances.

But if his wraith was projected into the bedroom of the Grand Hotel in Calcutta by him suddenly thinking of his nephew, and thus, by association, of his niece in Rangoon, moments before he died, further and more measured visits were prevented by the shock of his death and by the need of his separated conscious wraith to adjust to the spiritual realm in which it found itself. For sudden, violent death is often followed by a recuperative delay lasting several months or longer before the wraith is ready or able to communicate with the living.

Mrs Bowyer Bower, as her account, quoted in volume XXXIII of the *Proceedings* of the Society for Psychical Research, reveals, was not in fact contacted by her dead son until either the end of November or the start of December 1917. The first inkling she had of his coming was to see a yellow-blue ray of light which seemed to arise from the curtains of her bedroom, that next moved across the foot of her bed, and 'then came round right across in front of where I lay'.

'I watched,' she revealed, 'not at all nervously, and something like a crumpled filmy piece of chiffon unfolded and the beautiful wavy top of Eldred's head appeared, [it waited] a few seconds and his forehead and broad, beautiful brow appeared; still it waited and his lovely blue eyes came, but no mischievous twinkle, but a great intensity. It all shook and quivered, then his nose came. More waiting and quivering and then his tiny little moustache and mouth.'

From this description it is evident that Eldred's head gradually assembled itself from the spiritual precursor resembling 'a crumpled filmy piece of chiffon', which may mean that during the nine months of Earth time since his death Eldred had lost his human form in the next world, or that he had, at least, difficulty in manifesting in that guise in this one.

'At this point he turned his head very slightly and looked right into my face,' continued his mother, 'and moistened his lips slightly with his tongue. I kept quite quiet, but it quivered and shook so much and no chin came, and in my anxiety I put out my hands and said, "Eldred, I see you," and it flickered quite out, light and all.'

Three or four weeks afterwards, Eldred's wraith was able wholly to appear to his fiancée Æta Highett, who on the night in question, after having asked him to rap if he intended appearing to her, but who, on hearing two raps in response, then fell asleep when nothing thereafter happened. However, when she awoke a little later, Æta found his spectre sitting beside her on the bed, dressed in a blue suit. Bravely, she spoke to the apparition and it replied, she said, in a voice 'just above a whisper'.

'I then tried to touch him,' she added, 'but my hand went through him, and like a fool I started to cry, and he disappeared.'

Equally remarkably, it sometimes happens that only one particular but clearly recognizable facial feature of a departed loved one appears, which, like the respective parts of Eldred Bowyer Bower's face, does not have to form against a solid background, but can float independently in the air. This happened to Jill Eaton.

Mrs Eaton explained that on the evening when the incident occurred she was half sitting up in bed, her attention fully taken with listening to a phone-in radio programme. The time was about 10 p.m., the date Thursday, 8 July 1999, just over six months after her husband's death. The only light in the room came from her bedside lamp. Nothing had happened during the day to suggest that any sort of supernatural visitation was about to occur.

'But, suddenly, a small brown cardboard box entered my line of vision in the air space between me and the centre ceiling light, which was off,' she revealed. 'Behind this little box was the engine of a toy clockwork train set which I recognized as belonging to my husband.'

Jill knew that the actual box, whose visionary duplicate she could see, contained a new metal wheel for the replica engine which was floating behind it, a wheel that her late husband Alf, a model train enthusiast, had ordered and received, but which he had never found the time to fit. But what happened next was even more surprising.

'As these two items hung there, suspended in mid-air so it seemed, staring directly at me appeared my husband's eyes, his unmistakably large grey eyes, not his head, nor his face.'

Then Alf's familiar voice emerged from the eyes, saying, 'Do you know where that is?', and referring, Jill realized, to the hidden wheel. Despite being astonished by what she was seeing and hearing, Jill automatically pointed to the chest of drawers at the end of her bed, and replied: 'Yes, in there, bottom drawer on the left.'

'And with that,' continued Jill, 'the box, the engine and Alf's eyes faded. It must have been a matter of under ten seconds, if that. I remember feeling flabbergasted on realizing that he had actually been in the room with me if only extremely briefly; and at my own composure at the matter-of-fact way I had answered his question.'

Jill admits to feeling a bit miffed that her husband did not ask how she had been getting on without him, but puts the omission down to the fact that he must have known how she was coping, and thus didn't need to ask. But in case the cynic might wonder why he then needed to enquire about the whereabouts of a model-train engine flywheel, which has no importance at all in the grand scheme of things, we might reply that it wasn't the question that was important but the spiritual display of which his eyes and voice formed the crucial part.

'It was a strangely comforting experience,' said Jill reflectively, 'and most certainly nothing to be frightened of.'

Which is perhaps the reason why it occurred.

CHAPTER SIX

Voices and Other Sounds

When day was gone, and night was come,
All people were asleep,
In glided Margaret's grimly ghost,
And stood at William's feet.

from *Fair Margaret and Sweet William*, trad.

THE HEARING OF a departed loved one's voice has been reported on many occasions. The unexpected sound of such treasured tones is always, of course, a pleasant surprise in itself, but what is said invariably brings comfort to the bereaved along with the reassurance that, while the relative or friend is physically dead, his or her conscious other self survives in the next realm of being. Several words may be spoken to make a statement, impart a piece of advice, or give a warning or prophecy; or just the hearer's name may be called out, which may serve as a cautionary shout or as notice of the caller's death.

I referred in my book *Disembodied Voices* to Dr Samuel Johnson once hearing, when he was a student at Oxford, the voice of his mother, who was at home in Lichfield, Staffordshire, call out his name as he returned to his lodgings. His biographer James Boswell, who recorded the incident, then goes on to confide to us that 'An acquaintance, on whose veracity I can depend, told me that walking home one evening to Kilmarnock, he heard himself called from a wood, by the voice of a brother who had gone to America, and the next packet brought accounts of that brother's death.'

Another late eighteenth-century case involved an official at the Bank of England who, while dressing himself one morning at his lodgings, heard his first name called three or four times by the voice of his mother, although he assumed that it was his landlady's niece imitating her who was responsible. On going downstairs and mentioning the assumed fine mimicry to his landlady, he learned that the niece had been away from home since the previous day and that nobody, in fact, had called him. Shortly afterwards, while at breakfast, the man received news that his mother had died suddenly, which had occurred at the same time that he had heard his name called by her and, when he accordingly hurried to her house, he found her laid out 'but that when he saluted his departed parent, he saw her eyes open, as if to take a farewell of her son'.

A far more recent calling by name happened to Dorset resident Dorothy Wratten, whose husband Edward died in 1985, although his unexpected vocal contact did not take the form of an alert or a warning, but rather a reprimand.

A week after Edward's death, Dorothy retired to bed that night feeling very distraught, and she began crying for him, as she told me, in 'a desperate, destructive manner'. Then suddenly, to her astonishment, she heard Edward's voice from near the door call out 'Dorothy!' loudly and clearly in an admonitory manner, instead of using the endearment 'Darling' as had been his wont.

Dorothy was shocked into silence, and she remained tremulously hiding under the duvet before soon falling asleep. She woke the next morning feeling refreshed by her peaceful slumber, and she never again mourned for Edward in such a heart-rending way. He had told her, in no uncertain terms, that such behaviour was unnecessary and pointless, that she had to pull herself together and that, while he had died physically, he nonetheless still existed in the world of spirit. She should, in other words, be celebrating his continued survival, not lamenting a stage of existence which could only ever be temporary.

A Surrey man named Nigel B., a former member of the Society for Psychical Research, told me that he had often discussed with his wife 'the question of communicating with the other one as soon as it was possible in the post-mortem state'. They had, in other words, made a pact together, and after his wife predeceased him, dying as she did from a cardiac condition in late February 1992, Nigel hoped that she would soon get through to him, as promised.

But, as we have seen, the interval between a person's death and his or her moment of contact can be much longer than expected, particularly when the illness which caused the former is protracted, as it was for Nigel's wife. The delay, as I have said earlier, probably occurs because the departed wraith needs an extended period of rest to recover itself fully from the physical trauma it has undergone. Hence it was not until September of that year, some seven months later and when the initially disappointed Nigel had forgotten about their pact, that his wife was finally able to get in touch with him. It happened late one evening when he had fallen asleep in bed while sitting up and reading a book.

'I was woken up by my wife's voice calling my name in my *left ear only*,' Nigel told me, 'although both my ears were clear of the pillow.

'Her voice was a very strong, clear whisper: "*Ni-gee*". It was quite unmistakable. This was my wife's nickname for me over thirty years ago. It was a greeting she used to use when meeting me to give me some good news and when she was very happy. This was no dream. There was no ambient noise in the bedroom. My neighbours were away.'

The clear indication of her delayed greeting is that Nigel's wife wanted to let him know, with one uttered two-syllable word, to wit his name pronounced in a well-remembered, loving and familiar way, that she not only still existed but that she was happy and pleased to be where she was.

A much shorter period of time passed before Monica Boyce heard the voice of her late husband William. This might be because he had died in a hospice and so was perhaps more mentally prepared for the event. But, anyway, about six weeks after his death Monica was in her workroom one afternoon looking for something or other that she had lost, for she has never been, as I described above, very good at finding things.

'But then I heard William's voice call out "Monica" quite loudly from the living room,' she said. 'I was naturally astonished at hearing him call and it took me a few moments to realize that he was dead. His voice sounded so real and lifelike. I did go into the living room but William, of course, wasn't there. He had spent a lot of time in the living room reading before he went into hospital and then into the hospice, and if he wanted anything he would call me just like he did then.'

Monica says that this experience, which occurred when she was busy looking for something and not thinking about her husband, alerted her to the fact that he was still with her in a spiritual form even though he had physically died. And it gave her the confidence to start talking to him, as she had promised, on a regular basis, and was the reason why, when necessary, she would ask him for his help in finding lost items.

In *Disembodied Voices* I reported the remarkable experience of Jean Akerman, who lives at Porthcawl in South Wales. As a very young woman Jean had to travel all alone to London to undergo a long, difficult, lung operation. The day before it was carried out she went into the church beside the hospital to pray for divine assistance. Then, as she sat there and silently reflected on the ordeal which lay ahead of her, she suddenly sensed the presence of someone standing in the pew behind her, whereupon she heard a male voice say calmly and authoritatively in her left ear, 'Jean, don't worry, you're going to be all right. I'm going to take care of you.'

This unexpected uplifting statement was followed by the sensation of a hand being laid firmly and comforting on her left shoulder. Startled, Jean turned round immediately to see who it was but found no one there; nor was there anybody else in the church who could possibly have been responsible for what had happened. The kindly spiritual presence, which was perhaps her guardian angel or a similar divine being, had given Jean the reassurance she so badly needed. And, as it had promised, the operation turned out to be a complete success.

Many timely warnings have also been uttered by unknown voices, which may come from the dead and which have often helped saved lives, both of the hearers and sometimes also of their families.

A remarkable example of such a helpful voice was heard by Soffrey de Calignon (1550–1606) when he was the Chancellor of Navarre, which was then an independent kingdom in south-west France. He was roused from sleep one night (probably in 1594) by the voice calling out his name. However, as nothing further ensued, he presumed that he had dreamed of the waking cry and went back to sleep again.

Not long afterwards Monsieur de Calignon was again similarly woken, except that this time he was sufficiently impressed by the utterance to awaken his wife and tell her about it. She was naturally alarmed by what her husband had said but, when nothing further was heard by either of them, sleep again claimed them.

However, Soffrey de Calignon was disturbed from his slumbers by the voice for a third time. But, if annoyance was mixed with apprehension in the Chancellor's overwrought mind, he was next relieved to be spoken to, while awake, by the mysterious voice, which warned him that bubonic plague was about to break out in the town, that it would cause many deaths, and that he would be well advised to take his wife and family away to a place of safety. Not surprisingly Monsieur de Calignon followed the advice given (although it is not recorded if he warned his fellow citizens of the coming outbreak) and he and his loved ones were thereby saved from the deadly contagion.

The Chancellor did not know, of course, if the source of the voice was a dead person's wraith or ghost or if it was a spiritual entity in its own right. The former is perhaps the most likely, for wraiths do like to help the deserving living, even if they have never met in life. But it is evident that the entity concerned was not able to manifest as a semblance of itself, which rendered it impossible for Monsieur de Calignon to determine who or what it was.

An example of constructive advice given by a wraith is described in the article entitled 'Extraordinary Experiences of the Bereaved' by Louis LaGrand. The incident happened to a young woman, who told LaGrand that, on returning home from her father's funeral, 'she had gone upstairs to her room for a brief respite and as she closed the door she felt a hand on her shoulder and heard her father say, "Take care of your mother." His voice was as clear and convincing, she said, as though he was standing right next to her.' Here again, the touching hand is used to emphasize the importance of what was said and to bring home to the grieving daughter the fact that the afterlife is a reality.

Voices are by no means the only type of sound that can come from the beyond, even though they are generally the most arresting and moving. Quite often sounds that once were heard with the voices make the transition into our world with them, thereby helping the living hearers to understand what is going on.

Recently a correspondent, whom I shall call Samantha Moreton, wrote to tell me of a strange experience she once had on a hot, humid September night in 1973, when she resided at Biggin Hill in Kent. At around midnight, feeling uncomfortable and being unable to sleep, she sat up in bed against her pillow to read. Then, through the wide-open windows of her room, there suddenly came a noise which not only caught her attention immediately but which helped divert her from the stickiness of the night.

'The sounds which distracted me were those of a child's garden swing,' she related, 'squeaking in its to-ing and fro-ing; and of children's chattering and laughter, soft laughter, excited at their play yet quietly contained somehow.

'I would like to emphasize that the laughter had what I would call a beautiful quality, the like of which I'd never noticed before, and it was coming and fading, coming and fading, as if being carried to me and then away again on a gentle wind or breeze. But there was no gentle wind, nor breeze. The night was perfectly still with no air movement of any kind.'

As far as Samantha could determine, the sounds came from the garden belonging to an elderly couple living opposite her, who she knew had neither children nor a swing. Yet, when she went to the window to look out, the location of the sounds changed.

'They now seemed to be coming,' she said, 'not from the garden, but all around the general vicinity, still with an intermittent coming and fading motion. It was not in the least eerie because it was so happy and lovely to listen to.'

During the next couple of days Samantha made some inquiries about the sounds. She discovered that, while the elderly couple who owned the garden from which she thought the sounds had come had heard nothing, the old woman who lived next door to Samantha had heard them on several occasions. And this neighbour believed they came from the piece of waste ground that stood opposite her, next to the elderly couple's garden.

The empty plot had once belonged, she explained, to a London man who in the 1930s had built a wooden bungalow on it for weekend use. However, when the Second World War started, he moved into the bungalow permanently to avoid the bombing, and during the Battle of Britain he brought his grandchildren out to stay with him for their safety. Then one afternoon, when the children were happily playing outside, a German Heinkel III bomber heading for RAF Biggin Hill prematurely released its payload of bombs, one of which fell on the man's plot, killing him and the children, and demolishing the bungalow.

My correspondent had previously noticed some rotting wooden boards and rusting iron chains, like those of a child's swing, in the nearby waste plot, and speculated: 'I wonder if, what I heard on that humid Saturday night more than thirty years later, could have been some sort of supernatural recording or re-enactment of the events leading up to that fateful daylight raid all those years before.'

The same puzzlement about the origin of children's voices was felt by Paul and Sylvia Pearson not long after they had moved from St John's, Newfoundland (which was where Paul saw a ghost combing its hair in their bathroom mirror), into a smart, four-year-old suburban home at Sunnybrook, near Montreal.

'In the third bedroom, which we never liked and don't use, I can often hear a child crying,' said a mystified Paul. 'It usually happens in the evening and always when Sylvia's not home. But when I go up to find out what's happening, it cries until I get up near the bathroom and then the sound stops. Our son sleeps in the room opposite but it doesn't seem to bother him.'

While his wife has never heard the crying from the upstairs bedroom, she has both heard and felt some other childlike manifestations from much nearer to her.

'I keep hearing a child's voice calling "Mummy",' she told me. 'I thought at first it was our son but whenever I turn around there's nobody there. And often when I come back from the stores I hear a sound in the house like the murmur of voices, but as soon as I get in it stops. Then one night when I was meditating I felt a dead weight on my stomach, just like a child was sitting on me and nuzzling up to me.'

The couple told me they were sure no child had died in the house, but Paul wonders if he and Sylvia might be hearing ghostly sounds made at a much earlier time.

'After all, there could have been a farmhouse here back in the 1800s,' he speculated. 'We might be picking up the cries of some long-dead child.'

Even more spooky is the fact that sometimes a loud noise occurs, such as, for example, the smashing of bottles in a cellar or a kitchen, whose cause seems entirely clear, but when the damage is investigated it is found to be illusory, for no bottles have been broken. And, bearing this seeming impossibility in mind, I would like to mention one noisy happening of this type which once occurred in my own family. The phenomenon was heard (*c.* 1909) several times by my paternal great-grandfather's second wife-to-be, Rebecca.

Rebecca's romance with my widowed great-grandfather began while she was teaching at the Church of England school in Runton, Norfolk, of which he was the headmaster. During the pre-nuptial period she was lodging with a family in the village. The family, somewhat unusually, kept a number of old, unused iron bedsteads in their attic. And, strangely, every so often when those in the household were sitting in the living room, reading or talking, there would come a tremendous metallic crash from above, which sounded just as if all the bedsteads had fallen over. Yet, when the men of the family raced up to the attic to find out what had happened, nothing was seen to be out of place. All the bedsteads were neatly leaning together up there as usual.

Such ghostly loud noises have been reported on many occasions and it is impossible to say how or why they happen. They are certainly alarming to those who hear them, but are they really meant to frighten and intimidate the hearers? They may possibly have taken place without any reference to them. For, after all, why should we suppose that every supernatural event is performed with us in mind? To think like that is surely making obeisance to human egotism.

Moreover, where the bedsteads are concerned, we cannot know if they were really knocked over to make the noise and then hastily picked up again, or if the crash was merely an aural semblance created by the unknown ghost. And, if the occurrence was meant to be heard by those sitting below, was it simply a mischievous act or was it prompted by boredom? After all, it can't be much fun being confined in someone's attic!

The hearing of ghostly music at someone's death has been frequently reported and it is a far more friendly and enchanting way for departed spirits to acknowledge the arrival of a new member among their number, while at the same time giving comfort to the bereaved. The music may come as if from an organ, piano or a violin, or even on occasion from drums and flutes. Voices are sometimes also heard singing. Such music is invariably described as beautiful, and is sometimes hauntingly so. This does not always mean, however, that it is unrecognized.

For example, Helen Creighton mentions a lady at Victoria Beach in Nova Scotia who heard a spiritual choir singing a complete rendition of the hymn 'A Perfect Day', which seemingly came from a corner of the bedroom, when her brother, whom she was sitting beside at the time, died there. But when a man was dying at Ship Harbour, both he and his wife heard a violin being played, although she said, 'I didn't recognize any particular tune, just the sound of music and nobody anywhere near to be making it.'

CHAPTER SEVEN

Mists and Vapours

In the middle of the floor stood a black coffin –
there he lay in the quiet sleep of death: his wish
was fulfilled – his body was at rest, his spirit
travelled free.

from *The Galoshes of Fortune* by Hans Anderson

IT IS SOMETIMES reported that a deceased person makes contact by means of a smoke-like mist or a vapour. The mist may serve as an obscuring medium out of which a solid-looking wraith or ghost suddenly emerges and into which it eventually disappears, or it may act rather like a supernatural canvas from which, or upon which, a recognizable face or an entire form is generated as a visual representation of the departed. On other occasions an object or even an animal appears within the mist, in which case the mist may function as a forerunner. In my own experience, however, the smoke-like mist is how the departed person presents himself or herself, and is thus a way of making a visual appearance without having to generate a human form.

Joan Forman relates in *Haunted East Anglia* the frightening experience of a certain Mr Berry, a teacher at Oundle School, who one day returned after work to his lodgings in the village of Elton, to find what appeared to be a globular-shaped portion of mist on the floor of his room. The misty ball then began to roll around the floor, watched in fascinated horror by Mr Berry, until it reached the wall beside the fireplace, whereupon it rolled up the wall and settled itself on the mantelpiece. Then it transmogrified into the face of an unknown man, who regarded the terrified teacher for several minutes with an evil, bone-chilling stare, until both it and the mist faded away. It was a spectral manifestation without apparent point or purpose, unless it wished to let Mr Berry know that his presence there was not welcome. In this regard it was entirely successful in hastening Mr Berry's departure.

Sally Worth, the acrobatic dancer and roller-skater whom we met in Chapter One, told me about how she witnessed a mist one night which she at first feared might engulf her and which underwent a similar transformation. The uncanny incident took place in 1960, twelve years after she saw the double of her husband-to-be Peter, although the face that appeared in the mist was that of her dead father-in-law. Remarkably, it possessed the same very unwell expression that his son's double had had.

At the time, Sally and Peter were living at the top of a large Victorian house in Wandsworth, London, which they had formerly shared with Peter's parents. The lower part of the house was then occupied by Peter's unmarried sister Muriel, who had cared for their father Frederick in his declining years. Frederick had died, after a long illness, two years previously.

'I had gone into the bedroom that night to give my second son, who was just six months old, his late-night feed,' recalled Sally. 'When I had put the baby down in his carry-cot, I just leaned back against the pillow on the bed's headboard to rest myself and, as I turned my head to glance out of the door, I saw there a haze or mist, which was gradually coming towards me. I couldn't believe it. I thought, "What's wrong, what is this?"'

Sally said that outside the bedroom was a large landing, which had stairs and banisters leading up to the far corner, and that the mist came from by the stairs.

'It headed straight towards me, moving quicker and quicker, and came into the bedroom. I was leaning back watching it with my hands clasped in front of my chest,' continued Sally, who still finds it difficult to come to terms with what happened. 'And then suddenly a face appeared in it, which wasn't very clear at first, but then it was, although I didn't at first recognize it as that of my father-in-law Frederick, who looked so haggard and ill, so terrible. I could see part of his neck as well, but not his shoulders, and his grey hair, which looked a bit longer than I remember it being. And his face just stayed there, staring at me so intensely. I couldn't speak. I was very frightened. And then, suddenly, everything just went. The mist, the fog as you can call it, just went with his face.'

Sally still can't understand why the mist and Frederick's face should have appeared to her just after she had finished feeding her baby, especially as she had not been thinking about anything in particular at the time. Indeed, she had had a good relationship with both her in-laws, who she says were 'lovely people' and of whom she was very fond. Frederick, however, had been very ill before his death, which took place in hospital.

'I can't imagine why it should have happened,' she lamented. 'I've never experienced anything like it since and it's now been half a century since it did happen, but I can still remember it so clearly. So it remains a mystery.'

Her two psychic experiences, however, share a theme in that both men, father and son, were represented as looking very ill, which Peter certainly was at the time, whereas, while Frederick had been dead for two years, he had been in poor health beforehand. This may mean that Frederick's haggard appearance was meant to recapitulate that of his son, who had recovered from serious illness and started a new life with Sally, and so demonstrate that he, Frederick, had been similarly reborn into a new life, notwithstanding the frightening visage he was obliged to manifest.

Jill Eaton tells me that her mother had a broadly similar experience back in 1978, which happened shortly after she and her husband had finished renovating a cottage near Yeovil, in Somerset. The cottage was one of four which had together once been a large, eighteenth-century farmhouse with a staircase at either side of it. And her parent's cottage, being at one end of the row, contained one of those staircases.

Because it was tricky to draw the curtains in their bedroom, Jill's mother had taken to undressing in the dark, which as it happened gave her the opportunity to view the wraith that appeared, for it was adverse, as she later learned, to appearing in the daylight. Its coming was announced by a rustling of skirts from the staircase, which prompted Jill's mum to turn her head in the direction of the door.

'There she saw, to her utter astonishment, hovering on the threshold of the bedroom door,' writes her daughter, 'a hazy, pinky-red glow, which formed itself into the shape of a child's picture-book drawing of a Christmas tree. Above this mass was the shape of a woman's old-fashioned bonnet and gradually, as the thing advanced into the unlighted bedroom, it took on the shape of a woman in a frilly dress, plus bonnet and with a reticule over one arm.'

The fully formed ghost then glided across the room, went past the stunned watching woman, through a corner of one of the single beds, and then disappeared into the wall on the opposite side of the room. Her mother did not feel at all frightened by it, nor did she ever see it again, but she did hear the rustling of its skirts several times afterwards as it mounted the stairs.

Jim, her next-door neighbour, into whose front bedroom the ghost evidently went as it vanished through the wall, said that he had seen the phantom woman several times, but added, with a nice bit of Somerset humour, that as it had never tried to climb into bed with him, he wasn't much interested in it!

Yet, notwithstanding these dramatic manifestations, a smoke-like mist may sometimes appear, as I mentioned earlier, without developing any accompanying face or form, but is the visual impression itself. I have seen this remarkable phenomenon on many occasions and it resembles a very fine, wispy smoke, light grey in colour, which rises quickly from floor to ceiling.

When my mother, for whom I had been caring, died in 2005, I was as upset as any son would be. We had, however, seldom discussed supernatural matters as the subject rather frightened her, although I had, as circumspectly as possible, suggested on more than one occasion that, in the event of her death, she would, if she could, contact me from the beyond, and that, if I went first, I would do the same for her.

Two evenings after her death I was sitting in the living room feeling very distraught and staring tearfully into space. Then, suddenly, I noticed what at first I thought was a fine smoke, as described above, rising rapidly from the carpet all around me, which ascended to the ceiling and thereby filled the air of the room. And although there was no accompanying smell of burning, I immediately feared that a fire had started in the flat beneath, which presumably was by then well alight.

I jumped from the chair and dashed downstairs, only to find upon arriving at my absent neighbour's front door that there was not one wisp of smoke emerging from underneath it, no glow of flame showing through the glass panel above it, no odour of burning, and no detectable rise in circumambient temperature. A studied look from the outside through her bay window revealed a similar absence of combustion within. My neighbour's flat was thankfully not ablaze. So I went back upstairs feeling relieved, but very puzzled. It was only when I returned to the living room and saw that the strange, odourless, very fine, smoke-like effusion was still rising from the floor to the ceiling that I realized my mother was surely the cause of it. I believe I sat talking to it and surrounded by it for an hour or so, until it suddenly disappeared, leaving the air as clear as if it had never been there.

I have since seen the smoke-like mist on many dozens of occasions, although it never again appeared quite so extensively as it did on that first evening. I quickly accepted it as a psychic manifestation and, while I would have much preferred my mother to have appeared as a solid-looking wraith, I know that, for whatever reason, it was the best she could do.

There was no further sign of it, however, until the day of her funeral, five days later. Then, on that morning, while standing in the kitchen waiting to depart for the cemetery, I saw the mist reappear, this time in broad daylight and on the other side of the kitchen table, more localized than before but equally noticeable. As I wonderingly looked at it, it suddenly came into my head that I had not taken any of my hypertension pills since the day of her death. I had quite forgotten to do so, and it struck me that my mother had returned just then to remind me of the fact. I thanked her and made good the omission, then I set out for the cemetery.

The uprising smoke of my mother's wraith returned almost daily during the next few months, sometimes appearing as often as four or five times a day. This suggested that she had either not come to terms with being in the beyond and wanted to remain where she felt she belonged, or that she was worried about me and how I was coping. Since then the number of her visits has gradually fallen off, so that now I may only see her once a month or less, usually when some crisis or difficulty occurs.

The phenomenon, however, has since been augmented on occasions by the appearance of a second smoky mist, which always appears to the left of my visual field and which is thicker, brighter and more silvery in appearance. The fact that I cannot look directly at it and that it moves with my head, led me at first to think that it was an optical illusion. I have since become convinced, however, that it is spiritual in nature and perhaps represents my guardian angel, for it too is invariably helpful.

But a guardian angel is perhaps more often seen as an apparent full-bodied person, in which guise it will bring comfort to the person concerned and protect him or her from harm. The aforementioned Brenda Collins saw hers several years ago after there had been a spate of robberies in the Parkstone area of Poole. The perpetrators were two local men, whose method of carrying out their crime was for one of them to ring the victim's front doorbell to ask for directions or for some other apparently innocuous reason, and then, while the housewife was so distracted, his associate would slip in through the house's back door to purloin any handbags, purses or cash left lying about inside.

One day, Brenda saw these reprobates up ahead of her when

she was on her way to the shops. She immediately feared for her own safety and that of her handbag but, on looking about her in alarm, she saw that there was no one else in the road to whom she could appeal to for assistance.

'Then, to my surprise,' she told me, 'there appeared beside me from out of nowhere this lovely old gent with a white beard.

'"Oh my! where did you come from?" I exclaimed. "There was nobody in sight just a few seconds ago."

'"I am always here when needed," he replied. "I am always here. I walk this way all the time."

'"But I've never seen you before," I protested.

'"You have never needed to," he said.

'I asked him if I could walk with him and, when he said he'd be delighted to have me accompany him, I told him why I particularly wanted his company, to which he just smiled reassuringly. And as we walked I just kept talking to him, mainly about myself, I suppose, to which he answered by simply smiling so kindly and charmingly.

'We soon came up to those men who were loitering on the pavement, but they did not even notice us. I felt like I was invisible when we passed them. Then, when we got to the crossroads not far ahead, the nice old gent said, "You are safe now."

'I asked him which way he was going, and he pointed to one of the roads leading off from the junction. I thanked him again, to which he replied, "I am near when you need me."

'I only took two steps before I turned around to look back at him, and as I did so he disappeared right in front of my eyes. That's why I can say he's my guardian angel.'

Like Monica Boyce and the helpful assistance she receives from her departed husband, I soon found that my mother was perfectly willing and able to assist me in a similar way. For, if I was unable to recall where I had put something and had gone through the business of searching for it without success, my mother would inevitably appear in her ascending smoky form in the air of whatever room I was in. I realized she could see me and sense my frustration, and that she certainly knew where the *objet perdu* was. It was at that point, like Monica, I would ask out loud for her assistance, saying clearly, if exasperatedly, 'Please, mother, help me find—'. Her response was immediate and spot on, and given in one of two ways: either my eyes were somehow directed exactly to where the missing object was, or I suddenly knew where to look for it – out of sight in a box or cupboard, for example, or in another room. Books, spectacles, papers, and a whole variety of needed objects and mislaid items, have been retrieved in this way, for which I am very grateful.

Her assistance in this manner could be regularly relied upon during the first three years after her death, although her daily appearances certainly became fewer as time passed. And today, as I mentioned above, her visits have virtually stopped. This is due, in part, to the natural order of things for, while a spirit often does remain earthbound for some months or even years after its body's death, when it can be of service to the living, the time comes for it to move on and to progress spiritually.

But, although wraiths like being helpful, there are evidently strict rules about what they are allowed to do. My requests have at times unknowingly overstepped the mark, which is why my mother has got herself, I believe, into spiritual hot water for trying to do more than she is permitted to.

About nine months after her death I had the temerity to ask her if she would tell me, if she could, when I was destined to join her. There was no immediate reply but, after I had repeated the question, she replied to me as an inner voice, which succinctly said, 'You will be with me by the end of next month', which rather took me aback. March was the month in question. I repeated the request a few days later when I was out for a walk. Her clearly recognizable voice, speaking inwardly to me, gave me exactly the same reply. They are the only two times I have heard her voice. I was convinced by the pronouncements that my end was nigh and that I had to prepare for it. So I set about finding an executor, deciding who would inherit my cash and belongings, and writing a will: a tedious, time-consuming business, but necessary, I thought.

I went through that March feeling somewhat overwhelmed by all the extra work my mother had brought upon me, but became more cheerful as things got done and the meeting with my Maker approached. I was puzzled to note, however, that my mother's appearances abruptly stopped after she had given me the approximate date for my demise the second time. This robbed me of her support, although I did gain help and encouragement from a friend named Margaret whom I have known for many years and who trusted my judgement in such matters. I felt no fear, yet I did wonder how I would be taken. I presumed I would probably be run over by a car or suffer a heart attack.

As it turned out, I was wrong about both. My extremely close encounter with eternity actually took place at home, where towards the end of that month I had at least two hypoglycaemic collapses, hitting my head each time on the coffee table, and giving myself an extensive subdural haemorrhage. But, fortunately, Margaret telephoned me shortly after the last fall, realized I wasn't talking any sense, and called an ambulance. This led to me being quickly admitted to the Royal Free Hospital in London, which specializes in such matters, where I had my skull opened and the blood clot removed. Had I been left to my own devices, of course, I would have died, so that timely telephone call was a life-saver.

Was my mother therefore wrong? I am still here, but it was a very close thing. If she hadn't told me I would die by the end of March, I wouldn't have done all that preparatory work and thereby been in regular contact with Margaret, my old friend. And Margaret would almost certainly not have called me when she did. In fact, when it is remembered that the departed have great difficulty in saying even a few words to us, then my mother, knowing of the danger that lay before me and the fact that it should have been fatal, gave me a brief answer which allowed me unknowingly to manipulate events to avoid my death. I simply asked the question which allowed her to do that, which is incredible.

My mother appeared to me in the hospital after the operation in her misty form, and two or three times more when I was recovering, but once home there was a lacuna which lasted for several months. I now realize that she had broken the afterlife rules by warning me of my coming death, even if that death did not occur, and as a result was temporarily forbidden from visiting me. There are, it seems, certain things you are definitely not allowed to do as a spirit, one of them being, as Elizabeth's guardian angel told her, 'It is absolutely forbidden to tell anybody they are going to die'.

The wraith, as I discovered, is also very restricted in what healing help it is allowed to give; neither is it permitted, as I also found out, to bend the laws of nature.

Early in 2004 I developed a strange loss of feeling in my right hand, accompanied by coldness and a stiffness of the joints, which effectively put paid to my love of playing the classical guitar. Electrical tests revealed that the nerve to the hand was being compressed in the carpal tunnel, and this seemed to be the cause of the problem. But, while I had a corrective operation in late 2006 to relieve the pressure, matters did not markedly improve. My hand remained cold and lacking in sensitivity and in free movement.

Then, in February 2007, having been visited one evening by the smoky mist of my mother, I asked if she could do anything for my hand, reasoning that as conventional medical treatment had failed, she could perhaps effect a cure. I therefore held my afflicted hand in the uprising mist for about ten minutes, noticing as I did so that it felt as if some otherworldly influence was being applied.

My hand did feel somewhat better in the morning, and this improvement lasted, I was glad to notice, throughout the day. On being visited again that evening by the same smoky mist, I gratefully described to my mother the benefit I had received, but regretted the lack of a complete cure. I therefore asked for further help and held my hand out again into the uprising vapour. Again, my hand was mistily embraced.

That night the truly remarkable happened. I woke from my

sleep at about three in the morning and found that my hand not only felt warm and completely normal but that its flexibility had been fully restored. I got out of bed and stood up, noticing as I did so that I was able to move my fingers with all the freedom and rapidity they had once possessed, and aware that their sensitivity had fully returned. I had been cured, or so it seemed, by my mother's wraith. The improvement was absolutely astonishing. In fact, it was more than that: it was miraculous. How I wish I had gone straight into the other room and played a few guitar pieces to celebrate. As it was, after visiting the bathroom, I returned to bed overjoyed by what had occurred and looking forward to leading an unhindered dexterous existence again.

Alas, my hopes were not to be realized. I woke the next morning knowing immediately that the fantastic improvement had gone and that my hand was once more impaired, even though it was somewhat better than before. Thereafter things worsened until the condition was soon as bad as it had ever been. I realized why this had happened when my mother stopped appearing to me. She had quite obviously been told, despite her best efforts on my behalf, that such assistance to the living was forbidden, that she had overstepped the mark, and that she must suffer the consequences. Her visits for the next few weeks were accordingly cancelled.

Most recently her ability to find things for me was also taken too far. One night I wished to find a book in a box in a dark cupboard but was hampered in the search by having mislaid my black wind-up torch. The hunt for that necessary device became increasingly desperate, but the torch was, to my chagrin, nowhere to be found. At last I was driven by its absence to start removing the boxes from the cupboard yet again, when suddenly I noticed my mother's grey smoke-like mist rising swiftly in the air of the room. Her visits were by then infrequent, so I was very glad to see her again, particularly just at that moment. I immediately appealed to her for help in finding the torch, surveying the room as I did so in case my eyes should suddenly light upon it. They did not, but two or three minutes later, having turned back to the cupboard, I was astounded to see, reposing on the top of the white shoe box I had not long before taken from the cupboard and whose top had been completely bare of anything, the black torch, as visible as coal lying in snow. Its appearance there was wonderful beyond belief. It seemed quite obvious to me that my mother had moved it, or rather translocated it, from wherever it had been to the one place where I would be certain to see it.

The above incident took place at about 9 p.m. on the evening of Wednesday, 4 March 2009, but while it had a happy ending for me, my mother was not so fortunate. She had evidently done something else which was against the rules, to wit, translocating an object, as opposed to directing my attention to where it lay, for she was again stopped from visiting me. Indeed, I did not see any spiritual 'smoke' again until Sunday, 10 May, two months and a week later. I was sitting by the window in the early evening and listening to a pretty piece of guitar music adorned with bird song when I noticed the bright mist appear on my left side, informing me that at least that one was back. Rather later, after supper, while singing and strumming an old ballad entitled 'Slow Boat to China', I saw my mother's smoky mist rising, plainly visible, from behind the coffee table, where it continued to ascend for fifteen minutes. She had been allowed to return after that lengthy hiatus and was perhaps attracted into my presence by hearing me singing, after what had been for me an even longer break.

But, despite this, her visits were tailing off. She did not appear again until Sunday, 31 May, the fourth anniversary of her death. That evening I noticed the fine uprising vapour I associate with her coming from the polished inlaid wooden box, her youthful repository for treasured items, which sits at the centre of the coffee table, and from its immediate vicinity, before spreading itself to all over the table. The box and its contents might once have brought Adelaide Proctor's words to mind for her:

So now and then it is wisdom
To gaze, and I do today,
At a half-forgotten relic
Of a Time that is passed away.

The uprising 'smoke' was soon joined by the bright mist on my left, the two continuing for about fifteen minutes. This was, I felt, a goodbye visit, and indeed since then her visits have been brief and infrequent almost to the point of non-existence. Yet, thankfully, my guardian spirit still shows itself on occasions.

The other sensory impression from the beyond is the touch of an invisible hand, although tactile contacts are less frequently reported than those seen, heard or smelled. This may partly be because our skin is invariably overlain by clothing or bedclothes or is pressed against by some other tactile stimulus, which can make it difficult to distinguish the gentle touch of the hand of a wraith from the brush of material (or whatever) across it.

But wraiths do like to touch us, as the charming vignette quoted earlier about the child whose dead mother's wraith reached down to stroke his face reveals, as does the hand felt on the young woman's shoulder, which accompanied the sound of her father's voice. We must also remember that when curtains are drawn or other objects are supernaturally moved, such actions also involve an invisible, touching hand.

However, touch by itself is less useful than it might be because it is difficult for the recipient to tell who is responsible for it, and a clasping unseen hand may frighten the touched person, which is not the effect generally wished for by those on the other side. This is why the touching hand is often used either as an adjunct to a spoken voice, whereby it adds emphasis, or to guide the recipient's attention towards a particular location.

Andrew Lang quotes the woman who, having received some bank notes by post along with her other mail, later went to burn the letters, but who, upon making an effort to throw them into the fire, experienced the following.

'I distinctly felt my hand,' she said, 'arrested in the act. It was as though another hand were gently laid upon my own, pressing it back.'

On looking down in astonishment, the woman immediately saw that she had been about to throw all the money she had received into the fire instead of the letters. Her unknown spiritual helper, which may have been a dead relative or her own guardian angel, had restrained her action and had thereby prevented her from mistakenly burning the needed money.

Even more remarkably, a ghostly posterior may sometimes be used to alert a visited person to a spectral presence and to leave behind a visible impression at the place where it has sat.

When my late mother-in-law Emily lived at an old rectory in Rutland, where she resided for almost two years, she one night heard, long after she had retired to bed, and much to her alarm, the sound of her bedroom door being opened. Frightened, she lay there not daring to move and hardly able to breathe, while heavy masculine footsteps came into the room, accompanied by those of a middling-sized dog. The door was closed behind them. Emily then heard the man remove his coat, shake it and hang it up, and heard the dog shake itself too. The weather that night was bad, with gusting wind and rain, so there was nothing unusual about those actions, except, as Emily knew only too well, they were not supposed to be happening in her house and certainly not in her bedroom.

Once the unwanted intruder had divested himself of his coat, and the dog had started snuffling around looking for a spot to lie, the man approached the bed. Emily went cold with fear, her heart in her mouth. The man reached the end of her bed and then sat down upon it. She felt the weight of his body, the depression of the bedclothes and mattress made by him, and the pressure that these exerted upon her legs. She stiffened, expecting to be attacked at any moment. But, incredibly, nothing else happened. There was no further sound from either the dog or the man, and no movements. The room remained as silent as it had been before their unexpected entrance.

After lying terrified for several minutes, Emily eventually

summoned sufficient courage to extract her head from the bedclothes and to look at whoever was there. But no man nor dog was visible in the gloom. She reached out a shaking hand and switched on the bedside light. It too revealed that the room was empty of intruders, that no strange coat hung on the peg, and no wet footprints marked the floor.

Yet there *was* the impression of a man's backside on the bottom of the bed. So something had sat there, but why it did so on that particular night Emily was never able to fathom. The evident ghost and its dog were never heard again, although the rectory was apparently inhabited by other phantoms, ones not needing to take the weight off their feet!

I earlier mentioned Sally Worth's experience of having both the double of her sick former boyfriend Peter and, twelve years later, the ghost of Peter's father Frederick appear to her. Frederick's ghost unexpectedly looked as ill as had Peter's double, which itself reflected the bad physical shape Peter was then in. I bring up this again because Emily had often spoken of the phantom which had sat on her bed to her second daughter Anne, my wife's sister, who therefore became familiar with it. Now Anne had been disappointed by the fact that her mother did not make any contact with her after she died and wondered why this should be. But not all spirits can either get in touch as quickly as the living might like them to or in the clear, unambiguous way they would perhaps prefer.

Some years in fact went by before contact was made. Anne had by then grown up and was living, as an adult, on her own in her first flat, and was enjoying the independence and the freedom it gave. But then one night when she was in bed the unexpected happened. She suddenly felt somebody sit on the side of her bed towards its end. There was no mistaking the increased weight nor the accompanying pressure exerted on her legs by the downward pull of the bedclothes. And like her mother before her she lay breathlessly for several minutes, feeling scared and wondering what would happen next.

But nothing did happen next. There was no further movement or anything else to suggest that an intruder had gained access to her bedroom. So Anne too finally turned on the light and saw that the room was as it had been before she had earlier switched the light off, but that there was, nonetheless, the distinct impression of someone's backside on the bed's counterpane down towards her feet. There was no mistaking the indentation. The memory of her mother's long-ago experience came flooding back to Anne, and she realized, with almost complete certainty, that her mother had been the unknown caller, for by replicating what had happened to her she had thereby informed Anne of her identity.

CHAPTER EIGHT

Easing a Broken Heart

Beneath a church-yard yew,
Decay'd and worn with age,
At dusk of eve methought I spy'd,
Poor Slender's ghost, that whimp'ring cry'd,
O sweet O sweet Anne Page.

Slender's Ghost by William Shenstone

EVERYONE KNOWS HOW painful it is to be abandoned by someone you love. Tears and sleepless nights follow, which are made worse by the bitter realization that you have been rejected, that what you gave of yourself was not reciprocated, and that the continued sharing of hearts was an illusion.

Yet the end of a romance, while often deeply hurtful, is seldom entirely without hope. There is usually a glimmer of consolatory brightness in the gloom, a sense within oneself that the other might still realize his or her mistake, or that the choice you made was wrong, the promises you were given were insincere, and that your poor heart is more bruised than broken.

However, when death brings about the parting it is often unexpected, it is usually devoid of sour grapes, and it is attended by the finality of real loss. There is no possibility of returning to how things once were. The loved one has crossed the great divide, and the places that were once made joyful by his or her presence are now empty and echoing, bereft of the enlivening spark which gave them meaning. The future is darker, unwelcoming and seemingly pointless. Your heart lies crushed like a shell beneath Death's remorseless tread.

But while the dead are no longer physically with us, they have certainly not, as we have seen, gone altogether. The demise of the body sets free the soul form or wraith, the spiritual counterpart lying within it, along with the consciousness, from what was always their temporary home. Indeed, the wraith not only replicates in appearance its physical envelope (although it may sometimes appear to be several years younger in age), but it retains clear memories of its former life and of the feelings of care and concern it had for those left behind. The separation likewise sharpens its perceptions and gives it a fresh insight into its own failings and inadequacies. In this way the wraith becomes very aware of the part it once, perhaps unwittingly, played in causing the disappointments and unhappiness its family and friends may have experienced, and thus it develops far more sensitivity to their emotional plight.

It is salutary in this regard to realize that after-death punishment, as we might call it, is usually self-inflicted and arises from the deep anguish such heightened awareness brings to some wraiths. It is not – or at least not usually – meted out by demonic beings.

Such post-mortem insights and the regrets they may bring encourage departed wraiths to return, often remarkably quickly, to the material world, where they can meet and mingle again with those they love, who are viewed, so to speak, with fresh eyes. In fact returnees often spend more time with those they sense are hurting most, especially if they have contributed to that hurt, than they probably ever did in life. Wraiths without such guilt, while fewer in number, are still concerned about those they have left behind and wish to aid and support them.

But, although the returned wraith can see us and may relish being in our presence, it soon discovers that the barrier separating it from us, the interface between the worlds of spirit and matter, like the meniscus 'twixt water and air, is frustratingly one-sided, being clear to it but largely opaque to the living.

This is why, unless you are gifted with 'second sight' or psychic vision, you may have difficulty in seeing or hearing the returned wraith of your departed loved one, or indeed of even sensing its presence. But, nonetheless, do not let this stop you from speaking to, or asking questions of, him or her, or indeed requesting help when needed. For, while seemingly silent, the 'dead' are fully conscious, vocal and alert. But, because of the difficulty they face in getting through to us, it may take them some time to find a way of making contact. This is why answers to your questions may not come immediately and are seldom delivered verbally. But come they invariably do.

Contact is naturally made much easier if you believe, or are prepared to accept, that someone who has died, despite appearances to the contrary, is actually still here; indeed, your dismissal of the idea may be as painful to whoever has 'gone over' as his or her loss is to you. So your belief and your willingness to grant that death is not an end but a new beginning or rebirth, can blunt your own pain. It will help you understand that your loved one's physical absence is but part of both your stories. The real person within him or her has been released from a material world endowed with so much hurt, suffering and disappointment into the realm beyond of peace, laughter and joy. And, having taken the path that you will one day tread, he or she wants to tell you of the blissful life that awaits you, while wanting you in the meantime to grow in spirit, which often means abjuring those traits, attitudes and ways of behaving that are leading you to perdition.

We may wish to contact the liberated soul in a straightforward meaningful way, but this contact is hindered by the limitations imposed on all of us. The interface between our world of matter and the spiritual world beyond is unfortunately frequently impenetrable to our senses, or at best it is sporadically penetrable, which renders its inhabitants, who may be flocking around us, unseen, unheard, and unnoticed.

However, we must also accept the fact that some of those

who have passed on have no wish to make contact, while others cannot do so immediately because their experience of dying has left them exhausted and in need of rest and recuperation. As we have noted, several weeks, months or even years may pass before they are sufficiently restored to make the attempt, by which time those left behind may have forgotten about them or have pulled down their psychic shutters completely, thereby preventing contact altogether. Disbelief in the afterlife is likewise an effective damper, as can be modern society's lack of quietness and introspection. Present-day behaviour is often offensive to the dead for, having witnessed the tranquillity and loving kindness of the next world, few residents there actually relish stepping back into what seems to them like a ghastly, feverish nightmare.

This is why many people rely on various strategies to help them get over the heartbreak caused by death. One familiar antidote is to immerse oneself in a distracting activity, such as work or travel, or, more grimly, by replacing the lost loved one with an emotional substitute, such as membership of a golf club, a puppy, or even another partner. But grief is a necessary part of overcoming the pain of loss and should not be dodged or denied. And, while time is the great healer, any opening up to those extending a hand across the gulf separating us can make separation much easier to bear.

I have, however, already pointed out that a short spoken message may be swiftly imparted to the living. This happened, for example, when the deceased mother of a lorry driver named Yorkie, who had died one week before after a protracted illness, spoke to him in his bathroom. To his surprise, he heard her voice say clearly and distinctly, 'I'm all right now', which eased his grief and removed the anxiety he had been feeling about how she was getting on in the next world.

Psychic awareness can sometimes be enhanced by illness or injury, which is why reports of sightings of the dead given by people on the brink of death themselves are relatively common. The following is an interesting example of this.

While on board a Royal Navy warship guarding a convoy of food ships travelling from South America during the First World War, Lieutenant A. B. Campbell became witness to an interaction across the mysterious border between this world and the next. The incident occurred when a fatally injured fellow officer, surnamed Ray, whom Campbell, his best friend, had gone to visit in his cabin, suddenly rallied and introduced him to his brother Alec. Yet, as far as Campbell could see, no one else was there.

Lieutenant Ray had been in charge of the warship's port battery and had received his injuries when the gun, whose breech he had been trying to clear, suddenly backfired. At the time of Lieutenant Campbell's visit, he was by then barely alive, and Campbell, thinking Ray was hallucinating his brother's presence but not wishing to upset his badly wounded pal, rose to the occasion by contributing as best as he could to the talk that his comrade was having with his apparently non-existent sibling. Indeed, tea and biscuits were ordered for the three of them.

'I held imaginary conversations with Alec,' Campbell said, 'and at times almost seemed to feel that the fellow was really present.'

The wounded lieutenant died later that day. When the ship returned to Plymouth, its home port, Campbell regarded it as his duty to visit Ray's parents, whom he had previously met, and inform of them of the circumstances which led to their son's death. During their meeting he learned that earlier on the same dreadful day, Alec, their eldest son, who was an army officer in France, had been killed in action. This outcome further reveals that the wraith of the departed man was able to visit his dying brother almost immediately after his own death, when he could both be seen and heard by him, yet not by Lieutenant Campbell, his brother's friend and visitor.

The difficulty many have in sensing the presence of their deceased loved ones explains why spirit mediums are often asked to provide the necessary link. These psychically gifted individuals are reputedly able to 'see through' the interface between this world and the next and so act as go-betweens. Those consulting them can thereby often receive information about themselves which may be quite unknown to them and which would be difficult, if not impossible, for a medium to obtain fraudulently, notwithstanding the fact that some are charlatans.

In June 1923, author H. Dennis Bradley, who had previously published *Not For All* (1920), *Adam and Eve* (1922) and *The Eternal Masquerade* (1923), for which he had gained a reputation as a sceptical observer and cynic, visited New York, where he stayed with Josef de Wyckoff at his home, Arlena Towers, in Ramsey, New Jersey. His host, eager to keep the popular writer amused, asked him one day if he would like to take part in a séance, and Bradley, always ready to try something unusual and different, was amenable to the idea.

'I knew nothing of spiritualism,' the author remarked on his return to England, 'but it seemed a new way of spending an evening.'

H. Dennis Bradley heard his long-dead sister's voice speak to him

Wyckoff therefore invited to Arlena Towers an exceptionally talented 'direct voice' medium named George Valiantine, whom he claimed served as the focus for spirits of the departed, which were thereby able to produce their voices from out of the air and to which questions could be put directly. Most mediums, by contrast, have to go into a receptive trance during which the visiting spirit speaks through them, using their vocal apparatus, and whose voice, therefore, necessarily becomes altered to a greater or lesser extent depending on the facility and genuineness of the medium. The voices produced by a 'direct voice' medium, however, sound exactly like those of the deceased persons, for it supposedly is their voices that are heard speaking.

The séance took place in a darkened room, whose windows had previously been shut and locked and whose door was secured by means of a heavy piece of furniture pushed across it. The four sitters ensconced with George Valiantine were Josef de Wyckoff himself, his twenty-year-old nephew, a dinner guest named Joseph Dasher, and Dennis Bradley.

'For twenty minutes nothing happened,' reported Bradley. 'At first I was amused, and then bored.

'Then I heard a woman's voice, and I had to realize, after a few minutes, that my sister, Annie, who died ten years ago, was speaking to me. She spoke in an entirely characteristic way. I have never known any other woman speak in quite the same way. The voice exactly reproduced this peculiarity.'

The reunited siblings talked to each other for twenty minutes. It was a conversation that changed Dennis Bradley's life. He was entirely convinced of the voice's veracity and, as a result, that there is an existence after death. He had never seen nor heard of George Valiantine before and he knew that nobody in the room had the least idea that he himself had ever had a sister. It was therefore impossible that the voice could have been fraudulent.

'We discussed intimate points known only to myself and my sister,' he elaborated, 'with whom I was always particularly good friends. She said that she had been trying to speak to me for ten years, that she was perfectly happy, and that she was always with me.'

On the following evening another séance was held with George Valiantine, at which Bradley was able to converse for a further fifteen minutes with his dead sister, who likewise spoke to him 'from out of the air'. They discussed at some length various people they had once known and some occurrences in their lives which were personal to them. Even more surprisingly, ten other spirit voices were heard speaking that evening, and on later occasions, for Bradley invited Valiantine to England to sit for him there, the voices, both male and female, spoke fluently and unhesitatingly in a variety of different languages and dialects, including the better-known European languages, but also in Basque, Arabic, Hebrew, Aramaic, ancient and modern Chinese, Russian, Sicilian and idiomatic Welsh. Invited language experts and scholars who heard the voices testified to their unaccented naturalness, and that they were, in other words, being uttered by native speakers, not by George Valiantine, however gifted a linguist he might have been. And the voices divulged information known only to the hearers in these strange and exotic tongues.

Yet I can well understand that many people, having read that the séance was held in the dark, will maintain that some jiggery-pokery must nevertheless have been going on. Now I have been to séances where jiggery-pokery was certainly going on, and there are, after all, none so gullible as those who want to believe. At one séance I attended, for example, which was held in pitch darkness, two levitating rods coated with fluorescent paint, which were supposedly held aloft by spirits and so flourished gracefully around each other by them, were mistakenly clashed together by the clumsy but unseen human operators. This brought a gasp of dismay and a hurried apology from the medium, who explained that as it was the first time the spirits concerned had been to a séance, they were, as a result, unused to adroitly manipulating rods in darkness! Her rationalization was accepted without protest by those watching the charade.

But, although the suspicion of trickery would undoubtedly

remain if Valiantine the medium had always required darkness to perform, the fact is that he did not. Dennis Bradley eventually attended many séances with him which were conducted in broad daylight, in full view of the sitters, who heard the voices emerge several feet away from him in the air, but saw no movements whatsoever by his mouth and lips. The possibility of ventriloquism was also precluded by the fact that on several occasions Valiantine spoke to a sitter at the same time that the voice did.

The most decisive development occurred, however, when Bradley himself, along with his wife, developed 'direct voice' mediumistic powers themselves. 'I determined to experiment for myself,' he reveals in ... *And After*, 'and within a comparatively short time, after the first experiment in 1924, my wife and I succeeded in establishing communication in the "direct voice" with various spirits whom we had known on Earth, and who had passed over.'

It is of course easy to identify a spirit by the sound of its voice, if the voice, that is, is a familiar one, just as the features of a visible wraith or ghost, when clearly seen, are often immediately recognizable. Other forms of contact are less certain.

This is particularly true when such a supernatural contact happens in an unfamiliar environment, for then the clues as to who it might be are often lost. The personal experience outlined below is suggestive of an anonymous visitation of this type which was meant to reassure.

In early April 1997 I had a fall at home late one evening, which resulted in a bad cut to my scalp and, subsequently, a trip by ambulance to the local hospital.

Thus, at about midnight, I found myself lying on my back on a trolley in an emergency cubicle formed of curtained, wheeled barriers arranged against the hospital wall. The cubicle was about twice as long as the trolley and four or five times as wide. I was the sole occupant of this unusually large space, and had a drip in my arm. I was wrapped in a blanket for warmth and I had also managed to drape a hand towel across my eyes to shade them from the glare of the overhead light.

Although I could make out low voices coming from the next cubicle, where the patient was accompanied by his anxious wife, I was otherwise quite alone. Then suddenly, without any warning or any sound being heard, I felt the fingers of a small, very soft and gentle hand placed on the right side of my neck (which was about the only part of me that was exposed), where they remained for a few seconds. I felt them and their triangular shape clearly, for they were held together. Their touch was strangely wonderful, caring and soothing, but then, just as suddenly and silently, they were removed.

My first thought was that a nurse must have come into the cubicle without me hearing her and had touched me to see if I was all right. Yet when I hurriedly removed my free arm from the blanket and pulled the towel from my eyes to look around, I saw that there was no one there nor any sign that anyone had been there. A nurse would also have spoken to me, if she had thought I might possibly be unconscious, to try and prompt some reaction. I cannot guess why I was touched in that beautiful way, but it did tell me that I was not alone in a spiritual sense. Those angel fingers also augured, following some deftly applied stitches, my safe return home.

It is unfortunate, if perhaps understandable, that even when a wraith has appeared to a loved one following the death of its physical self, and when it is also able to speak and thus emphasize its continued survival, the visited loved one often fails to grasp the import of the contact. Margaret Gordon Moore gives a moving example of such blinkered resistance by describing the sad case of John Elson, a businessman who only acknowledged factual certainties, and who, as a result, never recovered from his wife Elvira's sudden death, despite her dramatic post-mortem appearance to him.

On the evening in question John Elson had given a dinner party at home for his new business partners, while Elvira had tactfully agreed to spend the evening with an old friend. But, when she had not returned by the time his colleagues departed, John Elson became puzzled at her lateness and somewhat concerned.

'Quite suddenly he heard a low sweet voice – his wife's,' writes Mrs Moore. '"John," she said clearly. "John ..." He looked up and saw her in her soft, clinging evening-gown, holding out her hands to him. "Listen, dearest," she said. "I was in a taxi, and it was crashed into by a lorry at a quarter to eleven this evening, but you must please believe I am alive, and don't grieve, darling." '

Elvira's image then vanished, and John Elson, jumping up, momentarily angry that his wife might have played a trick on him, was nonetheless soon quite sure that he had imagined the whole thing. But then his telephone rang. The caller was his wife's friend, her voice distressed, who gasped out the news of that tragic accident. He drove straight to her home, only to learn there that his beloved Elvira had been killed instantly, and was, according to his understanding of such matters, dead and gone.

'It did not occur to this shocked man,' says Mrs Moore, 'strong in his rejection of anything intangible or immaterial, that his wife had by the power of her great love been able to come to him at the precise instant of death to assure him that she still lived ... His heart was broken, and the comfort Elvira had endeavoured to give him failed to reach his inner self, because he would not allow it to do so.'

This tragedy clearly shows that the wraiths of the dead, when impelled by great love or great concern, can often immediately penetrate the barrier betwixt their world and ours, to bring an awareness of both themselves and their fate even to those loved ones who ridicule the idea of there being an afterlife.

Yet such disbelief in those so swiftly visited and their readiness to dismiss what they experience as the product of an over-active imagination or, perhaps, to the eating of a piece of cheese or a fragment of underdone potato, reduces the deceased's attempt at trying to make them understand that they are not dead, to nothing worthy of even their consideration. Such prejudice entirely blinds those afflicted to the glorious possibility that, lying beyond the pain and tragedy of this world, there is one where life continues and where love, joy and compassion are everything.

In contrast to such negativity I would like to mention the case of the wraith of a dead doctor named Bagnall who appeared to his mother and thereby had a wonderfully beneficial effect on her. The incident happened in 1953 and was collected by the indefatigable researcher Helen Creighton in Nova Scotia, where the Bagnall parents resided in the small community of Glace Bay.

The son had died prematurely and his parents had been rendered inconsolable by his loss, most particularly his mother. Then one day when they were sitting together at home reading, the mother sensed someone standing beside her and, looking up, saw her son there. Dumbfounded at the sight of him, she glanced impulsively at her husband but, finding that he had not noticed the young physician's presence, she again stared up at her son, whereupon he ran a hand through his hair, as he characteristically had done when alive, and smiled warmly at her.

'He did this twice,' Mrs Bagnall recollected, 'smiling each time. I was a different woman after that.'

Helen Creighton comments that while young Bagnall did not speak to his mother, 'His happy face was sufficient to assure her that grief was superfluous.'

The son then vanished, so that his father missed his visit, which seems to have been made especially to ease the pain that his mother was feeling, which was achieved. Indeed, as I have made plain above and as Dr Bagnall so clearly demonstrated, the physically dead want nothing more than to persuade those left behind them that what we call death is rebirth into a new life, where our existence continues without the rancour, hatred and strife that can make this one so bad.

My mother's brother Ken, in his later years, developed Parkinson's disease and by the summer of 1996 had been made very frail and ill by the condition. As he steadily deteriorated he was eventually admitted to hospital, where his wife and grown-up children regularly visited him. I was made aware that things had reached something of a crisis when my mother was telephoned by one of his two daughters on Thursday, 29 August to tell her that her brother was 'sinking'. However, I did not imagine for a moment that he was right on the brink of death, but thought that his demise might occur within the next few days.

That night I went to bed at about 11.40, where apart from reading for a while I wondered if Ken would contact anyone after he did die. The answer to that question came far sooner than I had expected.

On putting the bedroom light out, I closed my eyes and turned to lie on my right side facing the wall. But soon afterwards, just as I was drifting off to sleep, I was suddenly aroused with a start by what seemed to be a circle of influence, somewhat like a vibration but not a pressure, forming around my shoulders and upper back. It gave me a similar shock to that produced when someone creeps up behind you and suddenly takes hold of your shoulders. It lasted for two or three seconds, I suppose, and was quite unlike anything I had ever experienced before while half-sleep. It certainly woke me up and indeed somewhat alarmed me, although the general impression it gave was of someone playing a practical joke. And, strange to say, Ken in his younger days had liked playing practical jokes and having a laugh.

The following morning came the sad news that Ken had died in the night. I was startled that his death had occurred so soon. But once I had given my condolences to my aunt, I asked her what time he had passed away and was told that it had happened at 11 p.m., or about one hour before my unaccountably odd experience of the evening before. I therefore believe that Ken was responsible for my sudden waking and that he had chosen me, who lived over thirty miles away from him, to visit in his separated form because he knew that I was interested in such matters. I also believe that I prompted him by wondering if he would make such a direct contact.

CHAPTER NINE

Contact through Dreams

Which, you ask me, is the real life,
Which the Dream – the joy, or woe?
Hush, friend! it is little matter,
And indeed – I never know.

from *Dream-Life* by Adelaide Procter

MANY PEOPLE HAVE reported encountering a deceased loved one in a dream, which is generally a pleasant, if somewhat bewildering, experience for them. They tend, however, to regard the meeting as being 'just a dream' by which they mean that the occurrence was a bit of clever imagining concocted by their sleeping minds. Indeed, dreams have for a long time been regarded as self-induced phenomena by psychiatrists, phenomena which enable the mind, when asleep, to play out wished-for happenings, solve worrying problems, and indulge in sexual fantasies. This is why Sigmund Freud once called dreams 'the royal road to the unconscious'.

But if the human body, as I maintain, contains a spiritual simulacrum or double of itself, which can leave it during sleep, then many, if not most, dreams recalled on waking are probably memories of such nocturnal adventures, which include encounters with the wraiths of dead loved ones. If so, they allow the double and the wraith or ghost to meet on an equal footing, so to speak, especially as the dead, as I have pointed out, find it difficult 'getting through' to the living when they are awake.

Contacts made during sleep, however, have their drawbacks.

Scientific research has shown that, although virtually everybody dreams about four or five times a night, many people do not remember any of them (the so-called 'dream forgetters'), whereas others (the 'dream rememberers') perhaps recall only one or possibly two. Hence many dream meetings with wraiths are forgotten about completely, which must be very frustrating for the wraiths concerned. Yet it is also possible that most of these interactions are not really meant to be remembered by the waking mind. We know that the ancient Greeks and Romans believed that each spirit about to be reincarnated supposedly had to drink from the spring of Lethe or Forgetfulness before entering the body of an about-to-be-born child. This explains why few people can remember their former lives at all, let alone what happened to them during the intervening periods.

However, one documented and dramatic meeting which occurred between a double and a wraith did happen in ancient times. It was recorded because those involved were related to the documenter of the incident and because of the bizarre way in which it took place. And while the man to which the double belonged was not asleep at the time but unconscious, it was nonetheless a fascinating encounter.

The original narrator of the event was a first-century BC Roman polymath named Marcus Terentius Varro, who wrote a great many works – five hundred in all – of which only two have survived. That in which Varro describes the strange volte-face of his dying relatives was among those lost, but fortunately his account of it was summarized by Pliny the Elder in his *Natural History*. Pliny himself died in the volcanic eruption which destroyed the towns of Pompeii and Herculaneum in AD 78.

Varro's relatives in question were two brothers surnamed Corfidius, both members of the Roman equestrian order, or wealthy knights, of whom the eldest was Varro's uncle by marriage, being the spouse of his mother's sister. One day this man suddenly dropped down dead at his house. He was therefore laid out and his will read, which named his younger brother as his heir, who accordingly began preparing for the funeral.

But then, quite remarkably, the elder Corfidius, Varro's supposedly dead uncle, suddenly recovered his senses, sat up and clapped his hands together, thereby summoning his astonished servants to his bedside. He further astounded them by relating that he – meaning his spiritual self or double – had just returned from his brother's house, where his brother had just died, and whose wraith had begged him to take care of his much-loved daughter and had told him where he had secretly buried some gold. His brother's wraith had also insisted that he now make use of the funeral arrangements for himself instead.

While the revived elder Corfidius was relating these barely believable instructions, some servants of his brother ran in, their faces streaked with tears, shouting that his sibling had fallen down and died. This proved on investigation to be quite correct. And when the surviving brother went to his sibling's house he found the spot where the gold had been secretly buried, thereby affirming that what he said he had been shown by his brother's wraith was true.

There have been many accounts written over the years describing how a wraith has appeared to someone in a dream to help him or her solve a particular problem, usually of a financial nature, which has been worrying him or her. Some of these also date back to the distant past. For example, St Augustine of Hippo (AD 354–430), writing in the early fifth century, narrates how one Milanese man, having recently lost his father, was then unable to find written verification that his sire had paid a large debt, which it was now being demanded that he should settle. This caused him great anxiety, and also great distress because his father had told him nothing about the owed money. While in this agitated state he was delighted to meet his father, or so he supposed, in a dream, who thereupon told him that the debt has been paid and where the receipt he needed had been put. This enabled him on waking to find the document and so prove that the money had indeed already been paid and thus to expose the attempted fraud.

Yet, despite having had such a case presented to him, the saint was nonetheless rather piqued by the fact that his own deceased mother Monica, a fervent Christian, neglected to visit him in his dreams, noting that 'if the dead could come to us in our dreams then my pious mother would not fail to visit me every night'. And he lamented that he could not imagine how, after his mother had experienced the happiness of life after death, she would be so unkind as to refuse to console 'the son whom she loved with an only love' when he went to bed troubled by some anguish or unhappiness.

I am indebted to a female correspondent, who wishes to remain anonymous, for informing me about the next interesting case. It involved R.G., a former colleague of hers, with whom she had worked for many years, who was told of the whereabouts of a much sought-after item 'in a dream' by a relative who had died. It also nicely highlights the way in which those who are prejudiced against the existence of the next world will soon resolutely alter their views, like smokers who have given up the habit, should they have an experience of their own demonstrative of the contrary.

R.G., my correspondent told me, 'was so atheistic and so full of narrow-minded bigotry, that he would brook no argument from anyone that there was anything beyond this life. For years and years, when the subject came up at work, he would talk down anyone who dared differ with him and offer another point of view.'

But not long before her intolerant colleague retired in 1986 and despite his long and bitter opposition to anything to do with the supernatural, he confessed to her that the ghost of his long-dead grandfather, who had been a policeman when alive, had appeared to him in a dream in the mid-1970s to tell him where he could find his tattered and long-lost police notebook.

Grandson R.G. had a special interest in finding the old notebook because Edgar Lustgarten, the lawyer who had become a well-known broadcaster and presenter and narrator of films about criminal cases, wanted to make a television programme for the BBC on one of the cases that his grandfather had worked on and about which he had made notes. That case was the dreadful murder of an elderly shop-manager and his wife, surnamed Farrow, who ran an oil and paint shop in Deptford High Street, London, where they were killed in 1905. R.G.'s grandfather had not only been involved in the investigation but had arrested the perpetrators, who were two brothers, Albert and Alfred Stratton. They were in due course convicted of the crime and executed.

The notebook, quite amazingly, was found to be in the very place where his grandfather's ghost, as encountered by R.G. in his dream, had said it was, to wit, lying beneath a pile of assorted papers and miscellaneous oddments in the bottom drawer of a large Edwardian sideboard. It had probably been there, as my correspondent remarked, ever since 'the day grandfather changed into a ghost'!

'I'm afraid I couldn't resist the temptation to get a bit of "own-back" after all the flack we'd taken from him over the years', she went on, 'in the remark I made to him that it wasn't a ghost at all, but merely his own memory genes working overtime, reminding him of where he had seen the notebook during his boyhood years when he lived in the same house alongside that ugly old sideboard.

'That was mud in his eye all right – but would you believe it when I tell you that he got just as indignant and steamed up when arguing the reverse?'

It is of course very difficult for many people to take what happens in a dream as an actual happening, even though dreams can sometimes portray both past and future events.

St Augustine even reminds us of the well-known early Roman courtesan Acca Laurentia, who one day went to sleep in the temple at Rome dedicated to the deified Hercules. She dreamed that the god came to her and enjoyed her favours; he then told her that the first man she encountered on leaving the temple would pay her a fee which she should regard as a payment from him.

When Acca woke she naturally remembered the dream, but

was nonetheless startled to meet on leaving the temple a very wealthy old man named Tarutius. He was attracted to her beautiful face and voluptuous body, and shortly thereafter fell in love with her and made her his mistress. When he died not long afterwards, she inherited his money, land and property. So she was, in effect, amply rewarded by the 'dream' god for the pleasure she had provided him.

Ancient writers also tells us that Laodice had an equally startling dream in about 353 BC. She dreamed that the god Apollo joined her in bed one night and afterwards gave her a ring with an anchor engraved upon it, telling her to give it to her son as soon as he was born. What made the event even more striking is that, on waking in the morning, Laodice found a ring of this description in the bed, and that her son, whom she named Seleucus, was born with an anchor-shaped birthmark on his thigh and that all his descendants inherited the same birthmark. Seleucus became one of Alexander the Great's greatest generals and, hardly surprisingly, the commander of his fleet.

When bubbly carer Radha Bedessee, who was born in Guyana, came to England about forty-three years ago, she had a rift with her elder brother. This happened when she engendered his disapproval by behaving rather wildly back in the swinging sixties. And after her brother, who studied medicine and surgery in Britain, moved with the rest of his family to Ontario, Canada, leaving her behind, the split from him became wider and more or less complete.

During their years spent apart Radha's brother fell under the spell of an Indian guru, and when he retired from medicine he went to the sub-continent to live in an ashram run by the holy man, whose religion and philosophy of life he admired and whose meditative techniques he followed. He therefore became a believer in both the afterlife, as his Christian upbringing had taught him, and in the Eastern concept of the transmigration of souls. But sadly in 2008, while residing in India, the brother died without ever having made his peace with Radha or shown her that he had forgiven her.

However, on the night of the day he died, Radha had a remarkable dream about him, which occurred *before* she learned that he had passed away. She dreamed that she was lying asleep in bed, where she actually was, and that the two other beds in the room were occupied by her two other sisters, who were both asleep. She then, as it seemed, woke up and saw, standing at the foot of the bed, her long-lost brother. He looked much younger than he had been at his death, and younger than when she had last seen him, some years before. He wore casual clothes, and he seemed to be entirely well in himself, without any trace of the illness which had troubled him in his decline (he suffered from a heart condition). But, most importantly, he stood smiling warmly at her, with a calm, contented expression on his face.

Radha was overjoyed to see him, yet somewhat surprised at him being there and not entirely sure what was expected of her. So she lay there gazing at him, bathed in his smile and taking from it the feeling that he no longer felt angry with her or disappointed in her, and was, despite their long-standing rift, in a mood of both forgiveness and repentance. He wanted her to know that he had been wrong to turn his back on her and that she did not deserve the rejection she had suffered.

The pair remained gazing a one another, for 'a long time', as Radha said, possibly an hour. Then she closed her eyes again and fell asleep, before once more waking, into the light of her room, but without seeing her brother standing at the foot of the bed.

Radha rose with a wonderful sense of reconciliation in her heart and the realization that her brother had forgiven her. It was later that same day that the news came about her brother's demise. She was of course distressed by it, but having dreamed her dream she was nonetheless certain that he still lived in the next world and that they would, in due course, be together again there. Their parting therefore was only temporary.

Like those relatives and friends who make a post-mortem pact together, whereby the one who dies first promises to visit the other as soon as it is practicable, my late aunt and I, with whom I had often discussed the likelihood of there being a next world, had agreed to do the same. We believed that there is another existence after physical death, and we were both keen to do our bit in verifying the other's opinion on this important matter.

As it so happened, my aunt, who had the misfortune to contract MRSA in hospital after undergoing what should have been a routine operation on a stomach ulcer, went first, dying in November 1999. I was naturally upset about the manner and the suddenness of her passing, and of course sorry for her, although I looked forward with some anticipation to being contacted by her, which would certainly go far towards confirming my belief in the reality of survival. But there was no evident attempt by her to do that immediately, which was not surprising as everyone who suffers from poor health for a long time before dying (as she had done) requires, as I have mentioned before, a period of rest and recuperation before being able or allowed to make excursions to 'the Earth plane'. Two months passed before she did contact me, which in fact is a surprisingly short time, and her welcome arrival occurred in a way I had not anticipated.

At about one o'clock in the morning of Saturday, 19 January 2000, while asleep in bed, I dreamed I was sitting at my work table, which was in my bedroom, typing on my computer keyboard, doing some writing. There was nothing remotely odd about that, and I, as the dreamer, felt just as if I were physically sitting there. It was dark outside and gloomy in the room, although I had the table lamp on to enable me to see what I was doing.

Suddenly the telephone in the kitchen next door to my room rang. I remember wondering who it might be, but left it to my mother to answer the call. I heard her go to the phone and say 'Hello' and a few other words into it. Not long afterwards she called out to me, saying that it was my aunt Peggy, who wanted to speak to me. I stood up, feeling somewhat chagrined at being disturbed, and went out to the kitchen. The hall light and the kitchen light, as I expected, were on, but the telephone had been replaced, cutting off the caller. There was no sign of my mother. I therefore concluded that she must have become confused and had mistakenly put down the receiver.

I turned back, somewhat nonplussed, when suddenly, to my utter astonishment, I saw Peggy climbing the nearby stairs towards me. She was uncharacteristically wearing a white robe, long enough to reach down to her feet, which was distinguished by having what appeared to be epaulettes on its shoulders. These were quite narrow and flat with distinct forward- and behind-facing serrated (or zigzag) edges, from which the robe seemed to hang. I remember noticing that she climbed the stairs quite adeptly, yet holding the handrail with her left hand, while keeping the robe bottom away from her feet with the right one. She looked much younger than I remembered her and altogether more healthy and buoyant.

I was delighted by her visit and, when she reached the top of the stairs, I threw my arms around her, hugged her to me and exclaimed how marvellous it was to see her again. Yet, although she looked and felt entirely solid and real, I was at a loss to understand how she could possibly be there, as I was sure that she was dead. But then, having not long before had a book published about people who had mistakenly been buried or cremated alive, I immediately surmised that she must have been wrongly certified as dead and had regained consciousness in her coffin. From there, I presumed, she had been able to alert someone to her plight, and avoided being consigned to the crematorium incinerator.

This 'insight' had a dramatic effect on me as it woke me up with a start, and I found myself in bed, lying on my back with my head raised up on the pillows, from which vantage point another shock awaited me. For, as I opened my eyes and looked into the darkness of the room, I saw that, hovering a foot or so above my knees, was a shining, white, cloud-like shape, which was perfectly visible in the gloom. It was some two or three feet broad and about nine inches deep, and was gently moving by extending parts of itself outwards, which gave it an almost living motion. I regarded this opaque haze with wonder and interest, for I was sure that it was Peggy, who, while she had manifested as her recognizable self in my 'dream', along with the robe she wore, she was evidently unable to do this for me when I was awake.

I closed my eyes, suddenly realizing that our previous meeting must have taken place when I was out of my body in my double form, when I had been able to interact with her visiting wraith, but that now I was back in my body I was limited to the sight of her cloud-like self. This was, however, more compact and thereby more white and opaque than the rapidly uprising 'smoky-mist' materialization I later observed of my mother. I blinked open my eyes and stared at the gently pulsating shape again. It was an incredible sight, floating as it did silently in the air with a comforting grace. But, after watching its movements for some time, I suddenly felt tired and unresistingly allowed my eyelids to flutter closed. I was next pulled easily and quickly into the world of sleep, from which I did not re-emerge until it was daylight. The cloud had by then disappeared and I was fully back into the tedium of everyday 'normal' existence. My aunt, I knew, had kept her promise and I shall always be grateful for the way in which she did it. For, as she had shown herself in her human guise in my 'dream', I was naturally able to recognize her, which I might not have been able to do had she first appeared as a shining white cloud, remarkable though that was, when I awoke in the night.

This further demonstrates that many wraiths cannot manifest to us in their familiar human shape when we are awake. So, unless we have a particular psychic propensity, we are unable to see them around us. The situation, however, is different when our double separates itself from our body during sleep. This is why 'dream' meetings with the dead are far more common than those that happen when we are awake. Perhaps we thereby avoid the confusion which *might* arise if spectres could be seen as easily and as often by us when awake as are living people.

Helen Creighton writes of her cousin Marjorie who was regularly woken by an unknown figure appearing to her in her sleep when she worked in Bermuda. This reveals, as we shall see, that some wraiths will take it upon themselves to perform relatively mundane tasks which are of benefit to the recipient.

Marjorie, at the time, was employed as a clerk in one of the big hotels situated on the south shore of the island. She worked there every second night. This gave her plenty of opportunity to enjoy a game of golf in the afternoons, after which she would return to her apartment, have a shower and then lie down for a nap before either going to work or out to enjoy the night life.

And, remarkably, Marjorie's slumber was ended each evening at the same time, to wit, three minutes to six, when 'the figure of a woman with her hand upraised would come to her in her sleep, and waken her'. This enabled Marjorie to get to her job when she needed to be there. The figure never appeared in her dream sleep at any other time.

This helpful wraith or ghost, for such it must surely have been, performed this service for the six months that Marjorie was employed in Bermuda, and it seems to have been associated with her quarters, as it did not condescend to continue the job it had taken on once she had left the island and returned to Nova Scotia. And neither did Marjorie, it seems, try to discover anything about the death of the woman who was presumably its source.

Dr Creighton explains that Marjorie could not identify the mysterious visitor either, for 'she was never able to distinguish her features because all she ever saw was a shadowy form'. The dead woman therefore remained a figure of mystery, whose routine of rousing Marjorie from her sleep at 5.57 p.m. every evening probably derived from some similar commitment contracted while alive, which it helpfully transferred to Marjorie when it discovered she needed waking at that time.

Any wraith which is the victim of an unsolved murder has the greatest motivation of all to get through to the living to help bring whoever is responsible for its demise to justice. This may occur by the wraith appearing to its murderer and so frightening him or her into confessing his or her guilt. Alternatively, if the crime has not been discovered, it may show itself to a friend or a loved one and so alert him or her to what has happened, or it may play a more active and direct role in helping to solve the crime. Such ghostly occurrences are frequent in legend and literature, and I shall be considering several actual happenings in Chapter Ten.

Less well known are those cases which involve the wraith of a murder victim making contact with someone when asleep, through a dream, who can then help bring the perpetrator(s) to justice. A very early example of such assistance, even though the dream's initial warning, which might have saved the victim's life, was ignored, is narrated by none other than Cicero, the great Roman orator and writer (106–43 BC), in *On Divination*.

Apparently two wealthy travellers from Arcadia in central Greece, who were probably *en route* to Athens, had to spend the night in the city of Megara, which stands on the isthmus joining the Peloponnese to the northern part of the country. There, one of them stayed privately at a friend's house, the other in a public inn. The former traveller, having retired to bed for the night, was wakened in the early hours by a bad dream, in which his friend at the inn appeared and told him that the landlord of the inn was plotting to murder him and asked for his assistance. The man woke up and jumped out of bed in alarm but, on coming fully to his senses, persuaded himself that he had simply experienced a nightmare and so went back to bed.

However, on falling asleep again, it wasn't long before his friend appeared to him in another dream. This time he told him that he had been killed but hoped that, as he would not help him when he was still alive, he would not let his death go unpunished. The landlord, the ostensible dead man revealed, had concealed his body under a cartload of dung and was planning to have it removed from the walled city as soon as its gate was opened in the morning.

The man at the private house was suitably horrified by this unexpected nocturnal addendum and, having dressed himself, hurried straight to the gate, where he found a dung cart waiting to be driven through it. He alerted the gatekeeper to his mounting fears, and these were increased when the carter, noting the attention being paid to his cart, ran off in panic. The load of dung was thereupon fully examined and the dead body of the man who had stayed at the inn, to his travelling companion's great distress, was discovered underneath it. The discovery led to the landlord's arrest and to his subsequent execution for murder, his motive being robbery. Hence the victim's wraith gained redress for its murder, much to the wonder of the citizens of Megara.

An even more remarkable dream, in which the murdered man appeared to the dreamer to reveal to her both the identity and the whereabouts of the persons responsible for his death, happened in London at the end of the seventeenth century, some seventeen hundred years after that described by Cicero.

The murder and robbery took place on Saturday, 16 December 1695, at an inn in the parish of Cripplegate, in the east of the old metropolis. The unfortunate victims this time were the landlord, named Stockden, who was killed, and his housekeeper and relative, Mary Footman, who survived. The details of the crime and its astonishing aftermath were recorded by the parish curate, Richard Smithies, and verified by Dr Edward Fowler (1632–1714), then Bishop of Gloucester.

That evening Mr Stockden and Mary Footman played host to three rough-looking men, who arrived late and stayed late, notwithstanding Mr Stockden's desire to have them leave.

But then, quite suddenly, as Mr Stockden was sitting wearily in a chair, the trio, at an agreed signal, rushed at him and Mrs Footman. One of the men, named Mercer, bound Mrs Footman and forced a handkerchief into her mouth to stop her screaming, while the other two, named Maynard and Bevil, having taken hold of Mr Stockden, callously choked him senseless with a linen cord or cloth. Thereupon Bevil struck Mr

Stockden's forehead hard with the lock of a pistol, killing him. This vicious pair also wanted to kill Mary Footman but were fortunately restrained from doing so by Mercer. However, having committed the murder, they then robbed the house of its money and plate before making off into the night, leaving the traumatized Mary Footman behind them.

But not long afterwards a neighbour named Elizabeth Greenwood encountered the wraith of the murdered Stockden in her sleep, in what appeared to be a dream, and was taken by him to a house in Thames Street. This thoroughfare runs parallel with and close to the eponymous river, extending from the Tower of London, past Baynard's Castle, to Blackfriars Theatre. It was in this house that Maynard, one of Mr Stockden's murderers, was then lodging.

The next day the woman, showing exemplary courage, went to the house and asked for Maynard, but was told he had gone out.

That night Mrs Greenwood received another nocturnal visit from Mr Stockden in her sleep, who, evidently worried for her safety, told her that a wiredrawer, who were men of considerable muscular strength, must be hired to detain him. She therefore engaged one of these formidable fellows and his assistant for the sum of ten pounds. And together the burly pair managed to arrest Maynard, whereupon he was taken to Newgate prison.

At Newgate, Maynard, true to the honour of thieves, impeached his companions, naming not only Bevil and Mercer, but also another man named Marsh. While not having taken part in the theft and murder, Marsh had spotted the monetary potential in robbing Mr Stockden's inn, and had set the others up for it, thereby gaining a portion of the ill-gotten gains. As soon as he heard that he was wanted, however, he ran off.

That night Mr Stockden appeared to Elizabeth Greenwood in another dream, wherein he took her (again in her double form) to see a house in Old Street, which had two stairs outside, and explained that Marsh lodged there. The following morning the plucky woman went to the house, established that Marsh was still there, and ensured that, shortly afterwards, he was also arrested.

The same was done to Bevil, whose location on the other side of the river was likewise revealed by the murdered man's wraith in a dream. He, too, was sent to Newgate.

The last robber, Mercer, who had not taken part in Stockden's murder and who had prevented the murder of Mary Footman, did not become a subject of Mrs Greenwood's dreams, and thereby escaped with his life. His companions, however, were all executed.

Once that had been accomplished, Mrs Greenwood received a last nocturnal visit from Mr Stockden, who apparently said to her, 'Elizabeth, I thank thee, the God in heaven reward thee, for what thou hast done.' He did not appear to her again because, having brought his murderers to justice, he was then free to move on in the next world.

The murder of Maria Marten at Polstead, Suffolk, in 1827 is a notable and oft-quoted case. Its interest derives not only from the fact that it was solved by a thrice-repeated dream, but that the murderer later advertised for, and so found, a wife. The murder itself, however, was a sad, tawdry affair. The victim, Maria Marten, was a pretty, shapely and socially ambitious country girl, made pregnant by her lover, William Corder. She had his baby but it died soon after its birth, and she then, perhaps understandably, wanted Corder to marry her.

But Corder, the son of a wealthy farmer, while enjoying the delights of promiscuous sex, did not wish to burden himself with such an unacceptable union. For Maria (born in July 1801) was not an innocent virgin of whom he had taken advantage, but had already had an affair with his older brother Thomas, to whom she had borne a child some three and a half years earlier. She had taken up with William when Tom tired of her. This behaviour, as far as William was concerned, made marriage to her out of the question, and his widowed mother was also against the match. Yet Maria was insistent and driven, and had

William Corder's awful crime was revealed
by a repeated dream

the upper hand from a psychological point of view. Thus, pushed into a corner by her and seeing no escape, Corder finally arranged to meet her on the evening of Friday, 27 July in the ominously named 'Red Barn' on the family farm.

From there, he promised, they would travel together to Ipswich, where they would marry by licence, the ceremony being impossible locally because of his mother's hostility. Maria turned up, somewhat bizarrely clad in a suit of his clothes for disguise, but that was as far as she got. After a heated argument between the pair, mainly it seems about the burial of their child whose body Corder had simply disposed of, Corder cold-bloodedly shot and stabbed her. He then buried her still-warm body in a pit he dug with pickaxe and spade in a corner of the barn.

Astonishingly, Corder coolly remained at Polstead for several weeks afterwards, yet assuring Maria's parents that their daughter was now happily married to him but was staying out of sight at a safe distance, to avoid their union becoming the subject of local gossip, until the harvest was over and he might take her abroad. But finally, in early September, having threshed the harvested barley for his mother and stored the grain in the Red Barn, he declared himself unwell and said he was leaving for the Continent to seek a cure and to establish a home for himself and Maria. Then he mounted his horse and headed for London. Nobody, it seems, saw him go.

Corder next wrote to Thomas and Ann Marten, Maria's parents, informing them that he and Maria had gone to the Isle of Wight. This declaration temporarily satisfied them until Ann Marten, Maria's stepmother, dreamed in March 1828 a disturbing dream on three consecutive nights. In it her daughter's spirit took her into the Red Barn and showed her the dreadful events that had taken place there on the night she was last seen, thereby revealing her murder, and pointed out the exact spot where she had been buried in the now grain-filled edifice.

These dreadful night-time disclosures eventually led to the barn, when it had been emptied of its contents, being carefully searched, and Maria's poor decomposing body being found by her father Thomas at the place revealed in the dream. It was identified from the female clothes that it wore, for Maria had evidently removed Corder's borrowed suit before her death.

William Corder was eventually tracked down to a house in Ealing Lane, near Brentford, where bizarrely he was not only running a school for young ladies but happily living with a schoolmistress named Mary Moore, whom he had met by advertising in *The Times* newspaper (then a commonly used method of finding a partner) and whom he had subsequently married.

The fugitive was brought to trial and justice was suitably served when he was found guilty of Maria's murder and executed by hanging at Bury St Edmunds, before an immense crowd, on Monday, 11 August 1828. A portion of Corder's skin, suitably tanned, was displayed in a leather shop window in Oxford Street for many months afterwards. The rope used to hang him was sold for one guinea an inch, and the sum thereby raised more than covered the cost of his incarceration, trial and execution.

CHAPTER TEN

The Wraith as Crime Solver

The gentle ghosts of injured innocents
Are known to rise, and wander on the breeze,
Or take their stand by the oppressor's couch
And strike grim terror to his guilty soul.

from *Lines Occasioned by a Situation in a Romance*
by Henry Kirke White

THE PREVIOUS CHAPTER ended with a description of three historical cases in which the wraith of a murder victim, shortly after the
demise of its physical self, appeared to a friend or relative in a
dream and gave him or her information which allowed the crime
to be solved and the murderers punished. This perhaps shows that
the wraiths of the murdered are aggrieved by what happened to
their physical bodies, that they resent being so suddenly torn from
life and their loved ones, and that they are anxious to have the
murderer(s) brought to book and justice done. It also implies that
the wraiths of murder victims have a keen sense of right and
wrong, and that they certainly will, when at all possible, assist
those still alive to identify and find their killers.

Not all murder victims, however, are able successfully to
interact with the living when they are asleep, in what we call
dreams, for it seems that a personal relationship is required for
this to occur. The two parties have to know each other and thus
have a mental bond.

Wraiths have particular trouble communicating with those

who deride the supernatural and close off their minds. After all, it takes two to tango and if one partner thinks the dance floor does not exist, then the dance necessarily goes unrealized. This is probably why many wraiths or ghosts of the murdered dead will, when possible, show themselves by making a direct 'full-bodied' appearance, whose presence can hardly be overlooked or doubted, as Julius Caesar's ghost did to Marcus Brutus. William Shakespeare represents the latter as saying:

> The ghost of Caesar hath appear'd to me
> Two several times by night: at Sardis once,
> And this last night here in Philippi fields!
> I know my hour is come.

Such encounters were frequently described by the ancient poets and this antiquity gives an indirect suggestion of their reality. We can conclude therefore that some wraiths of murder victims are able, without the necessity of speaking, to impart awareness about their death or their place of death to the living, who may then be able to have their killers punished.

One mid-eighteenth-century murder revealed by a manifesting ghost happened near the small town of Knutsford in Cheshire, on a tract of ground known as the Higher Town Common. This large area of heath was crossed by tracks which gave access to those dwellings lying within and beyond it, from which rents had to be collected by the rental agent, who would often stop at an inn there to quench his thirst on returning with said monies.

On one occasion when the agent did this, however, he was never seen again, much to the distress of his family and his employers, who were left wondering if he had decamped with the cash, which was a considerable amount, or had been robbed and murdered. But, because no clue about what had happened to him came to light, the affair remained a mystery.

However, many years later, the inn landlord, who by then was retired, wealthy and well respected, one night got very drunk with some friends, and they had to help each other home through a part of the heath which lay near to his old inn. As they passed a particular sand hole, the landlord was suddenly greatly distressed to see the ghost of the agent appear before him, which made him cry out that the man had been murdered and that he lay buried in that piece of ground. His friends, who could scarcely believe their ears, tried their best to calm him and managed to lead him away.

The following day the landlord, having returned to his senses, excused himself by blaming what had happened on the drink he had imbibed. This satisfied his friends who, while nonplussed by what had taken place, had been too drunk to ask themselves why the rental agent's ghost should show itself to the landlord but not to them.

Three or four years later the landlord, who had never properly recovered from the shock of that night, was brought by ill-health to his death bed. As he lay contemplating his entry into the next world, the ghost of the dead man again appeared to him, this time at his bedside and bearing an ugly wound in the heart inflicted by the knife which had been thrust into its physical self. The landlord, driven nearly mad by the sight, immediately confessed to the murder, telling the parish vicar that, being greedy for the money the man had possessed on that night long ago, he had encouraged him to drink excessively and then had stabbed him to death as he was leaving the inn. He afterwards buried the corpse in the sand hole.

A search of the sand hole was accordingly quickly made and the half-preserved body of the rental agent was there found, with a stab wound in its heart. Hours later the landlord died, his guilt proved and his reputation in tatters.

So the murdered man's ghost, despite taking a long time to accomplish its mission, had frightened its killer into confessing his guilt, and had thereby cleared up the crime, solved the mystery, and sent the landlord to the beyond with his name besmirched by the knowledge of his vile deed.

A murder that was followed by a far more rapid visitation from the beyond, whereby the male victim's wraith appeared to a passer-by who recognized him and who was thus alerted to the man's fate, took place in colonial Australia, where it is today one of the modern country's best-known supernatural occurrences.

There is even a festival held each year in the town where it occurred to celebrate the remarkable event. Yet, while the 'full-bodied' wraith of the murdered man, whose name was Frederick George Fisher, was seen, it has regretfully ever since been called 'Fisher's ghost', which has led to it being depicted as a childish, Hollywood-style white phantom with large black eyes, which demeans the original experience and sadly renders it ridiculous.

Moreover, it has proved difficult to establish the facts of the case because the different printed accounts about it are at variance with one another.

But it is known that Frederick Fisher, the murdered man, began his life in London, England, where he was born in August 1792, and that he grew up to make a respectable living for himself as a shopkeeper. But in 1815, at the age of twenty-two, he was found to be in possession of some counterfeit money. This was a serious offence, and Frederick attempted to explain his ownership of it by claiming that the forged bank notes came from the payment of a debt owing to him and that he had had nothing to do with their illicit manufacture. The jury at his trial, however, was not convinced by his plea of innocence, and Frederick was accordingly sentenced to be transported to Botany Bay, in New South Wales, Australia, for fourteen years. He was shipped out to that faraway spot on Wednesday, 26 July 1815, one month before his twenty-third birthday.

Frederick Fisher survived the long voyage, and upon arriving in New South Wales he adapted well to his new environment, worked hard and responsibly, and gained the approbation of his custodians. In 1822 he applied for and was granted a legal ticket-of-leave, which gave him the freedom to live a normal life and to advance himself as actively as the next man.

He settled in the small community of Campbelltown, situated

amid farmland about thirty-seven miles from Sydney, where he was granted thirty acres of land, which by industry, thrift and sober living, he managed to turn into a successful working farm. He also managed to buy another farm and several houses. But, to confuse matters, Penrith has also been named as the place where the murder and its supernatural aftermath occurred. And there is some evidence that he fell into debt and was pursued by one of his creditors, which ended in him having to endure another short custodial sentence.

It was prior to this incarceration that Frederick became closely involved with George Worral, a friend and neighbour, whose surname is sometimes spelled Worrall or Worrell (and who is also sometimes known as Thomas Smith!) Worral proposed that Frederick should make him the temporary owner of all the property in order to prevent it from falling into the hands of Frederick's creditors, and that he, Worral, would return it to Frederick once the debt had been paid.

But on the evening of Saturday, 17 June 1826, shortly after his release, Frederick Fisher unaccountably disappeared. It wasn't long before the locals began asking questions, and Worral told them that Frederick had not only left for England but had put the property into Worral's care until his return. When pressed, he showed papers purporting to have been signed by Frederick stating as much. The situation did not surprise most of his neighbours as they knew how much confidence Frederick had in Worral and of his oft-mentioned desire to revisit the old country to see his family and friends.

But not everyone was happy with the situation and murmurings grew among the Campbelltown populace, especially when Worral moved into Frederick Fisher's house and began selling Frederick's farm stock and other items belonging to him, although he claimed that he had been given power of attorney in such matters and that he was acting in Frederick's best interests. And although Worral was taken in for questioning by the authorities, nothing could be proved against him, so he was released. The waiting for Frederick Fisher therefore continued.

Adam Lindsay Gordon, Australia's greatest poet, perhaps gave the uncertainty of the matter its finest and most apt expression when he wrote in 'The Stockman's Last Bed':

> His whip at his side,
> His dogs they all mourn,
> His horse stands awaiting,
> His master's return;
> While he lies neglected, –
> Unheeded he dies;
> Save Australia's dark children,
> None knows where he lies.

A major breakthrough happened a few months after Fisher supposedly went to England, during which time the Honourable Alexander M'Leay, the Colonial Secretary, offered a reward for the recovery of Fisher's body (if dead) or for proof of his actual departure from the colony (if living), which went unclaimed.

Now, according to the anonymous lengthy article entitled 'Fisher's Ghost' which appeared in the March 1853 edition of *Household Words* (whose author was probably the Australian writer and poet John Lang), the breakthrough came when an elderly neighbour named Ben Weir drove home from Sydney by cart one evening six months after Frederick had disappeared (which would date its occurrence to about mid-December 1826, at the height of the Australian summer). As Mr Weir neared home he suddenly noticed a man sitting on the top rail of the wooden fence running alongside the road, whom to his astonishment he soon recognized as Frederick Fisher.

'The night was very dark', states the *Household Words* article, 'and the distance of the fence from the middle of the road was, at least, twelve yards ... He pulled his old mare up, and called out, "Fisher, is that you?" No answer was returned; but there, still on the rail, sat the form of the man with whom he has been on the most intimate terms. Weir – who was not drunk, though he had taken several glasses of strong liquor on the road – jumped off his cart, and approached the rail. To his surprise, the form vanished.'

Acting with commendable thoughtfulness, old Mr Weir then marked the place where the wraith had been sitting by placing some crossed sticks on the ground underneath the fence. He would thus be able to locate the exact spot again.

However, in the first version of the story, which appeared in a Sydney magazine called *Hill's Life* in 1832 and was anonymously written in verse, there are mentioned three people who see the wraith of Frederick Fisher sitting on the fence – albeit this time some four months after his disappearance, or mid-October 1826 – two of whom are boys, of whom no more is heard, and the other is a young farmer named John Farley, who is likewise returning home from market. Farley is portrayed as being stunned to see Fisher there, and Fisher is not only sitting on the fence but is pointing towards a creek (or, as in some later versions, at the pond) set some way back from the road. So Farley too stops his horse and cart and calls out to Fisher, but on receiving no answer gets down and walks towards him. And, as Farley approaches the missing man, Fisher is likewise reported to have gradually faded away before mysteriously vanishing into the night air.

Up to this point the two versions of the tale differ mainly in the names of the persons taking part in them. It is difficult to account for these name changes, which are completely pointless but, as I point out in *Supernatural Disappearances*, they are so common in this type of story that they present almost as great a mystery as the disappearances themselves, whether spiritual or physical. But, while the youthful Farley sees Fisher's wraith only once, and pointing, Ben Weir gets to see it again one week later.

This happened because, on returning home, Ben Weir found that his wife did not believe that he had seen anything which could not be explained away by the alcohol he had drunk. Annoyed by her doubt, Ben resolves that, when he goes to market on the following Thursday, he will not drink anything that day. And, true to his word, the old man not only stays sober but is not disappointed either for, as he nears the same spot on his return home, he again witnesses, as he had anticipated, Frederick Fisher sitting on the fence. But, lacking the Dutch courage that alcohol would have given him, he is too frightened to stop. This second sighting, however, assured him that what he saw was neither the real man nor an effect of drink, but Fisher's ghost. From that moment he is certain that Fisher is dead.

In both versions of the story a person of some authority in Campbelltown is next approached and, accordingly, a series of steps are taken which eventually lead to the discovery of Fisher's body. Aboriginal trackers are involved in the hunt, who among other things detect marks of 'white man's blood' on the fence where Fisher's wraith had been sitting, and then, by noting the slight remaining signs on the ground, are able to follow the trail left by the body which has been dragged, by its cotton necker-chief, away from the fence by the assailant.

The skill of the Aboriginals (whose leader, according to Lang, is called Johnny Crook) is further utilized to find the spot where the body has been hidden. In one version of the story, it has been dumped in the pond and kept submerged there by having a rock tied to its neck, and in another it is found buried some forty yards up the creek supplying the pond with water.

The discovery of Frederick George Fisher's corpse led to the arrest of George Worral and to his subsequent trial for murder, at which he defends himself vigorously, but is nonetheless found guilty of the crime. The execution day is set, as most executions then were, for the Monday following the verdict. This gave Worral the preceding Sunday to reflect upon the enormity of his crime, and to spend time with the prison chaplain, the Reverend William Cowper, to whom he made a full confession.

He had, Worral said, killed Frederick Fisher, whose property he coveted, by striking him over the head with a tomahawk after drinking with him in Campbelltown on the evening of 17 June 1826. This act was carried out when they were walking back together to Fisher's farm, at the place where the murdered man's wraith was later seen. He greatly regretted what he had done, and feared the fate which awaited him in the next world.

The felon George Worral was executed by hanging at Sydney on Monday, 19 February 1827.

There has been considerable dispute over the years about 'Fisher's ghost'. Was the spectre actually seen by John Farley or Ben Weir, or was it fabricated by one of them, and might he somehow have been involved in the killing himself? Or was the wraith simply a piece of creative fiction dreamed up by John Lang? However, the writer of the *Household Words* article, who claims that what he wrote is 'true in substance, if not in every particular', says that the murderer, while making his confession, swore that he had killed Frederick Fisher at the spot where his ghost was later seen. He would surely not have written that if the confession contained no reference to Fisher's wraith being seen after death.

The opponents of the supernatural version of the story are mainly those who disbelieve in life after death and who therefore cannot accept that such an entity as a dead man's wraith or ghost exists, let alone one that sits on a fence to alert a passer-by to the fact of its physical self's murder.

Yet, while it is impossible at this late date to be certain about what actually did happen, the cases discussed beforehand certainly show that plenty of wraiths and ghosts *have* been seen after the death of their physical body. This means that it is entirely possible for Frederick George Fisher's apparition to have been seen, especially as the man's violent death at the hands of one whom he regarded as his friend provided sufficient motivation for it to manifest to someone who would be instrumental in bringing the murderer to book.

One helpful, if unknown apparition was responsible for bringing about the rescue of a man who had accidentally fallen into a deep pit. The incident, which predates the murder of Frederick Fisher by about forty-two years, bears some resemblance to it, for the phantom, in an approximate prefigurement of Fisher's ghost, was first seen sitting on the bank of excavated earth thrown up around that hole in the ground.

The drama began on Sunday, 21 December 1783, when the unfortunately named John Thomas, a 62-year-old resident of St Just in Cornwall, left nearby San Crete to walk home. The time was seven o'clock in the evening, so it was very dark, the weather was cold, and John Thomas, an habitual drunkard, was sufficiently inebriated to find the act of walking along the rough path more difficult than he had anticipated.

'As it was dark he missed his way,' wrote William Moore, a resident of Redruth, who interviewed John Thomas after his remarkable rescue and who recorded his strange adventure, 'and about midnight fell into a pit about five fathoms [or thirty feet] deep.'

Such pits, many of which were dug over the years for the extraction of china clay or tin, are a hazard in the area and caution is still needed when in their vicinity, which naturally means rigorously following the paths leading between them. This John Thomas omitted to do.

When it was realized the following morning that John Thomas had not returned home, some of his friends set out to look for him, but their painstaking search proved unsuccessful. They were hampered by the fact that nobody knew quite where to look, and that the area was large and dotted with pits, boulders, stone walls and ditches. When nothing further was heard of the missing man, it was quickly assumed that he must either be sleeping off the effects of his carousing somewhere or had died – whether by accident, natural causes or murder.

But then something quite extraordinary happened.

'The next Sabbath day, as one of his neighbours was going to seek his sheep,' expounded William Moore, 'he saw, at some distance, the appearance of a man sitting on the bank which had been thrown up in digging the pit. On drawing near he saw the apparition go to the other side of the bank. When he came to the place he could see no one; but heard a human voice in the bottom of the pit.'

Mr Moore presumably had a full account of the phantom figure, which was far more marvellous to the locals than the survival of John Thomas for a week at the bottom of a pit, for he adds that 'it is said that several other persons saw the apparition, but took no notice of it'. Yet because, as we have noted, phantoms were given little credence by the educated in the eighteenth century, he says the bare minimum about it.

The opportunity for other passers-by to view the apparition came about because the man who first heard Thomas's voice at the pit bottom assumed it came from liquor smugglers who were hiding their ill-gotten gains down there. This prompted him to carry on looking for his sheep, for he did not dare to be seen by the smugglers, who were quite prepared to murder those who might betray them. The hiatus thereby gave the chance for others to pass by later, but they, as William Moore mentions, decided likewise to ignore what they had seen and heard.

However, when Thomas's neighbour eventually returned homewards and passed the pit again, 'he now listened more attentively, and as he could hear but one voice, he concluded it was John Thomas who was missing, and on calling him, he found he was not mistaken'.

A rescue mission was then mounted and a bruised, battered, chilled and barely alive John Thomas was in due course lifted, groaning and shivering, from the thirty-foot-deep hole, where he had been confined for a week. But, while close to death, he survived that long because there was fortunately a rill of a fresh water running through the bottom of the pit, which provided him with enough water to save him from dying of thirst.

No one knows whose wraith or ghost was kind enough to loiter at the top of the pit to mark it out for special attention, thereby enabling John Thomas to be saved, for William Moore does not record if it was recognized by any of the men who saw it. But the fact that they were certain it was an apparition suggests as much, despite the fact that most seemed to have ignored it or, as seems more likely, to have given it a wide berth.

CHAPTER ELEVEN

Souls in Crisis

But natheless, whilst all the lookers-on
Him dead behight, as he to all appeared,
All unawares he started up anon,
As one that had but of a dream bene reard,
And fresh assayld his foe.

from *The Faerie Queene* by Edmund Spenser

FEW SOULS THAT pass to the next world are without blemish, for in this life we are all fallible and prone to temptation. Thus we thereby fall into error, doing things that we know to be wrong, and which, if we had our time again, we would not do. It is our misfortune as humans to be motivated by greed and selfishness, which drive us remorselessly on towards that imaginary island called Self-Satisfaction, where we think happiness lies. But happiness, like God and the soul, has always resided within ourselves, and searching for it in the world around has us chasing after mirages, which offer nothing but frustration, angst and disappointment.

But when some people die who have done wrong in their lives, something distinctly odd then happens to them. They are not set free but are hamstrung by their wrongdoings at the place where their lives were passed. This stops them from moving on into the wonder of the beyond. Their situation is the direct opposite of those who return after death to help their relatives, lovers and friends. This is why they can be called souls in crisis, and they encompass, by and large, those apparitions which inhabit particular places, whether indoors or out. They may thereby engender real fear, which might lead to them having to be exorcized.

The other group of unfortunates, whose apparitions may be seen loitering in a particular spot, are those people who died when they least expected it, who had not, in other words, made any preparation, psychological or otherwise, for the event. They may not even have thought about such an apparently grim occurrence happening to them.

The young are particularly prone to unanticipated departure, for death seems a remote possibility to them, one lying too far ahead to be worthy of serious consideration. Yet they are just as vulnerable to illness, accident or crime as are adults, and it is these mishaps which not only kill them but result in their wraiths causing upset to the living.

In Chapter Three I wrote about the strange experience of the young Clarence Hearsey, who on New Year's Eve 1934 had the misfortune to see the wraith of his recently dead father standing looking at him from the top of a flight of stairs leading up to the servants' quarters of the family home at Maymyo, in Burma.

Some years later, at age twenty-one, Clarence became friendly with two men, Samuel and Fox, neither of whom was liked by his mother, for she regarded them as wastrels and ne'er-do-wells. This led to a disagreement between mother and son, and Clarence moved into the then-disused servants' quarters, where the wraith of his father had appeared. The ominous relocation was heightened one night by Clarence seeing the figure of his father, who had bandages hanging down his arm and who was holding a knife in his right hand, standing by his bed. His parent's post-mortem visit seemed to him like an omen of his own death.

The dramatic nature of the dream-like visit prompted his mother to urge Clarence to visit an astrologer and mystic to have the event interpreted, which he did along with his two disreputable friends, the oldest of whom, Samuel, a married man, was angry with Clarence for having gained the affection of a girl he loved. His jealousy led Samuel viciously to attack, rob and murder Clarence when they returned together across some empty fields. Clarence's skull was fractured with a heavy bolt and he was stabbed eleven times. His cries for help, though heard by people living at the fields' borders, went unheeded, and he eventually died.

One night a year later, however, Clarence's ghost was seen clad in white running through the same field. The sight was witnessed by the cook from a nearby girls' hostel and by his friend as they walked back across the fields from the local cinema.

'I saw a young sahib in white,' revealed the cook. 'He was beckoning to me with outstretched arms and asking me for help. "Help, help", his words seemed to echo across the damp fields. I turned to my friend and asked him to come with me, but he seemed rooted to the spot. I then handed him my lantern and umbrella and went to aid the young sahib, but something seemed to envelop me and I don't remember any more.'

The cries were also heard at the hostel, and the manageress there, remembering how they had ignored Clarence's pleas before he was murdered, sent servants out to investigate. To their surprise they found the cook running wildly about the field shouting for help. His body, it seems, had been possessed by the spirit of Clarence, in which, his wife supposed, it would stay for as long as they remained working at the hostel.

'Usually, the spirits of the dead return to their home and their loved ones,' explained Clarence's mother Ma Ma Lay to her daughter, 'but in this case Clarence returned to the place where he was murdered. When a life is cut down tragically, the restless spirit haunts the place where it suddenly left the body.'

Two years afterwards, Clarence's seventeen-year-old brother Willie was about to go to Mandalay to enter the Police Training School there, but before he was able to do so he contracted cerebral malaria and was choked to death when his brother-in-law foolishly gave him some rum to drink while he lay semi-conscious in bed. Willie's unhappy spirit thereupon became the most restless of them all.

His body was brought back to Maymyo, where the funeral was held. This obliged his Buddhist mother to feed the seventeen Buddhist priests, one for each year of Willie's life, who conducted the ceremonies as custom required, but in contravention of Willie's Christian beliefs. The family were of course very upset by the tragedy, as evidently was Willie, for once the Buddhist priests had left the house some unusual disturbances began.

That night, as his mother Ma Ma Lay and his two young sisters lay asleep, they were suddenly awoken by the dogs barking, which was followed by loud thumps and knockings coming from Willie's bedroom. His frightened family huddled together until dawn when the unaccountable sounds gradually subsided, yet when the bedroom was then examined nothing was found to be out of place. Indeed, all its doors and windows were locked and bolted.

The following day the devout Ma Ma Lay asked a Buddhist priest to conduct a ceremony to lay Willie's troubled ghost, for such was the assumed cause but, despite the *phongyi* chanting prayers all night, the racket became even worse. The windows rattled loudly as if blown in a gale, heavy thumps came from within Willie's room, and phantom footsteps strode around the veranda. These noises, combined with the relentless chanting, made sleep impossible for all concerned.

The next day the exhausted priest blamed his failure to quieten Willie's ghost on the dead youth's disbelief in Buddhism. He refused to try again.

The succeeding night was even worse, despite the presence of an army sergeant, a neighbour, who came to the house when the ensuing noises disturbed his pregnant wife. He did not believe in ghosts but could find no explanation for the sounds.

When the sounds started again on the fourth night, the sergeant insisted that the police be called. Two armed police officers eventually arrived at the house and they heard the sound of feet not only running around the veranda but also walking about on the zinc roof, as well as loud banging and the rattling of windows in Willie's room, but they could not identify what was causing it all. Hence they concluded that a supernatural entity which was beyond their ability to influence or control was responsible. They accordingly recommended, somewhat incongruously, that a night watchman should be employed to watch the house.

The Gurkha gardener was asked to perform the task. He left the next morning saying he would not do the job for another night for triple the money.

On the sixth night a Muslim Pathan servant was hired to watch the premises. He had a bed placed beside the window that had been wildly shaken but, despite his readings from the Koran and his generally fierce disposition, nothing changed. The banging, rattling and sound of footsteps continued. The Pathan's parting advice when dawn rose was that someone more skilful than he should be quickly engaged to cajole Willie's restless spirit into leaving.

So, in desperation, Willie's mother agreed that a Christian priest should be brought to the house to say prayers for her troubled dead son. Reverend Griggs of the nearby Baptist Mission House agreed to perform the service, and at ten o'clock that night, when the anguished noises again started, he, accompanied by Willie's sisters Amy and May, and a friend of theirs named Minnie, said the Lord's Prayer together, sang Willie's favourite hymn, 'Jesus Wants Me for a Sunbeam', and prayed for his soul to be at rest. Reverend Griggs then spoke to Willie like a son, explaining the upset and distress that the noises were causing to his family, and asking him to desist and go in peace. He next told the girls to go to bed and try to get some sleep.

'We had such faith in him,' writes May Hearsey, 'that we did exactly as he said, and soon settled for our night's rest, and to our utter relief we heard no more of the dreadful sounds that had disturbed our sleep for the past seven nights.'

Some readers may wonder whether this evident poltergeist manifestation was caused, not by the deceased Willie's spirit, but rather by one of his teenage sisters, to wit, May or Ruby, who were still living at home. (Amy, who was married, had only recently returned there.) This is not to say that either May or Ruby deliberately caused the mayhem, for this was demonstrably not the case, but rather that the unspoken inner hostility that one of them perhaps felt towards their domineering mother, who ruled them strictly according to the dictates of the time and who practised a different religion from them, may have unconsciously generated a psychic force sufficiently powerful to create the unfortunate disturbances.

Parapsychologists give the name 'psychokinesis' (or 'mind-movement') to the mind's ability to act directly on the nearby environment in this way and so make changes to it. Moreover, they maintain it is only negative emotions like hate, resentment and frustrated sexual yearnings which are sufficiently strong to produce noticeable effects like noises and furniture movements. Such emotions, it is therefore believed, are the ones that can manifest as a disruptive, damaging force.

However, this is a Western supposition that is based on the discountenance of the reality of wraiths and ghosts, and particularly those that may be unhappy with their lot. But Willie had every reason to be aggrieved at what had happened to him. Deprived by disease of his policeman father and two elder brothers (the eldest of whom, John, had died of cholera), he had at age seventeen just gained the chance of entering the prestigious Police Training School in Mandalay, when he was not only struck down by a serious illness but was killed by the stupidity of his sister Amy's drunken husband, who tried to pour rum down his throat. And when, after death, he found that nobody at home could see him or hear him, it is perhaps hardly surprising that he behaved like a distraught teenager and rattled windows, banged on the walls of his bedroom, and ran around its veranda and on the roof, whose sudden easy access must have been very tempting to him. But, unlike an outraged living teenager, he broke no windows, disturbed no tiles, and hurt no one. He just made loud noises to express his frustration at what had happened

and to let his mother know that he took his Christianity seri-
ously. He did not want Buddhists or Muslims reading their
prayers for him; it was Jesus, he knew, who wanted him for a
sunbeam, not Siddhartha Gautama or Mohammed.

Between the years 1807 and 1820, just over one hundred
years earlier, there occurred on the island of Barbadoes (as it
was then spelled), which was then part of the British West
Indies, a remarkable case of spiritual restlessness and seeming
anger that remains, for many, a daunting enigma to this day.
For in an otherwise perfectly ordinary, well-maintained graveyard, coffins lying within a specially sealed vault were
mysteriously displaced, broken and upended, which terrified
the locals, who were at a loss to explain who or what was
responsible for the outrage. And while no generally acceptable
materialist explanation has yet been given, the mischief is,
when viewed in the light of what has already been discussed,
completely understandable.

The frightening series of disturbances took place in the
cemetery adjacent to Christ Church, built in the seventeenth
century on the hundred-foot-high headland composed of
ancient coral, at Oistin's Bay, where a number of vaults had
been constructed in the rock. And it was within one of these,
which was bought in 1724 for the interment of the Honourable
John Elliott, that the mischief occurred. Yet his body was never
laid to rest there.

The modest vault, created from stone blocks cemented
together, lying partly above but mainly below the excavated
coral shelf, and fronted by a flight of steps leading down to its
door, was left empty for eighty-three years and did not receive
its first occupant until Friday, 31 July 1807, when Mrs
Thomasina Goddard, a married daughter of John Elliot, was
laid to rest there. The ownership of the vault then passed to
Colonel Thomas Chase, who first used it to inter his youngest
daughter, a baby girl named Mary Anna Maria, on Monday, 22
February 1808.

Mysterious coffin movements in this sealed Barbadian
vault caused general alarm

The vault was not again opened until Monday, 6 July 1812, after a passage of just over four years and four months, when Dorcas Chase, Thomas Chase's much older daughter, became its third inhabitant. It is relevant to note that no disturbance to either of the previously interred coffins was noted, and all seemed entirely normal within the vault, whose heavy bluestone marble door-slab had been cemented in place and required both masons and the strength of several black labourers to move and open it.

However, when Thomas Chase died two months later, great surprise and consternation occurred when the vault was opened to receive him on Sunday, 9 August 1812, for it was discovered that the coffins of Thomasina Goddard and Mary Chase had both been wrenched from their places. That of Mary, which, though small, was lead coated and quite heavy, had seemingly been tossed into the north-east corner, where it now stood upside down, whilst that of Mrs Goddard, which was made of wood, had been thrown for several feet and lay skew-whiff, split and partially open. The large lead-coated coffin of Dorcas Chase, however, had not been moved at all.

But, despite the chaos, it was decided by the Chase family that the interment of Colonel Thomas should go ahead anyway, for it was difficult to know what else to do in the circumstances. The two upended and damaged coffins were therefore placed back in their former positions, and the Colonel's coffin was laid reverentially beside those of his daughters.

The disruption had naturally alarmed the superstitious Barbadians who had opened the vault, and caused great distress to the mourners present, for it was completely unexpected. The former, moreover, were held responsible by the church officials, who said they must have surreptitiously entered the vault after the previous interment and caused the upset; and the Barbadians, despite vehemently protesting their innocence, were nonetheless reprimanded for it.

Yet there were also suspicions that others might be behind the disorder, because the burial of Dorcas Chase within the vault was by no means uncontroversial. Indeed, some on the island objected to her body's presence there at all, for the girl had apparently killed herself. The church officials, who felt them-selves to blame for allowing both the interment and the shameful desecration to occur, did their best to hush up the affair and to prevent news of it from spreading among the island's black population, but that was an almost impossible task.

Although there was no visible sign that the vault had been broken into, it was naturally wondered why, if any outraged objectors had managed to gain access, they left Dorcas Chase's coffin alone but had moved and damaged the one which had nothing to do with her and that holding her infant sister. Had hers perhaps simply been too heavy to shift, or might those who had entered, particularly if they were negroes, been too excited, nervous and hurried to know what they were doing?

The departing mourners must have surmised that if the interment of Dorcas Chase had been controversial, the situation was surely made worse by the addition of Thomas Chase. For his death had come about as a consequence of his deeply troubled and unhappy daughter's sad demise. The bitter remorse and profound depression that this caused him had also prompted him to make away with himself. A razor had done its ugly work. Thomas Chase was therefore the second suicide admitted into the Elliott vault.

It was then a felony to kill oneself, although a verdict of death by temporary mental derangement was often returned to excuse the act, which was not entirely false in the case of Dorcas and Thomas Chase, for both her personal unhappiness and his intense grief are forms of mental derangement. Yet everyone knew that the Order for the Burial of the Dead stated that the service shall not be used for those who 'have laid violent hands upon themselves'. This instruction was clearly contravened by those *felo de se* victims being deposited in a vault built on consecrated ground.

The next time the vault was opened was four years and forty-six days later, on Wednesday, 25 September 1816, and it took place for the interment of another baby, named Samuel Brewster Ames, the child of Dorcas's married sister. Over four years had gone by since the burial of Thomas Chase so, while everyone in attendance waited with bated breath for the vault's bluestone marble slab to be moved aside, nobody really expected anything similar to be witnessed again. How wrong they were!

This time all the coffins in the tomb had been moved, upturned, overturned and damaged, so that it looked as if a violent, malevolent wind had somehow blown through the vault and disturbed everything.

The shock and horror that this caused was genuine and the excited emotions they aroused quickly spread throughout the small island colony. Wild speculation was rife. Nobody could tell what was going on. Had the desecration been done by someone in the English community, angry that two suicides had been given a home in their graveyard, or had it been caused by some malignant spirit, which was the general view among the black population? Or were some so-called 'bad blacks' to blame, who were working off their jealousy and sense of inadequacy in this mean, underhanded way? Everyone seemed to be actively whispering and pointing fingers at possible culprits.

But then, on Sunday, 17 November 1816, less than two months after his nephew died, Samuel Brewster himself was called to join the other corpses in the family vault. The suddenness of his death and the accompanying freshness of the memories brought an expectant crowd out to watch the event.

They were not disappointed. When the vault was opened more disruption was discovered. The coffins had been thrown around again, including that of the most recent addition. Yet strangely, the coffin of Thomasina Goddard, the vault's first inmate, which had previously been so badly damaged by misuse and by insects that it had practically fallen in on itself, was untouched. It lay where it had been placed, tied up with cords, the shroud and body of Thomasina partially visible through the several splits and cracks in it.

Again the damage and disorder was patiently cleared up, albeit with trembling hands, and Mr Brewster was placed inside. The stone door was once more closed and sealed, and the crowd dispersed, but few islanders thought that the occupants of the tomb would remain at peace. After all, Samuel Brewster had not had a peaceful death. Indeed, the poor man had been brutally murdered by his own slaves. Hence his spirit could hardly be expected to take what had happened to its physical body lying down.

The next interment did not occur until Saturday, 17 July 1819, nearly three years after that of Samuel Brewster. The continuing general interest in the vault and its mysterious disturbances not only resulted in a large crowd gathering, but persuaded the redoubtable Lord Combermere (1772–1865) to follow the coffin, of a Mrs Thomasina Clarke, to what would hopefully be its last resting place, although nobody supposed that she would get much, if any, rest. At that time Lord Combermere was the Governor of Barbadoes and commander of British Forces in the West Indies. He had previously been commander of cavalry in the Peninsular Wars, and was, moreover, second-in-command to the Iron Duke at the battle of Salamanca.

The funeral thus gave this distinguished soldier the opportunity to witness for himself the gross disturbance within the vault when it was opened, for once again the coffins were seen to have been shifted about, upended, thrown against the walls, and generally mistreated. And when Lord Combermere had seen the unimaginable disorder, he told the attendants to straighten everything up and carefully to inspect the vault for any sign of a secret passage leading into it. When no such passage was discovered, for the walls of the vault were built of bonded stone blocks which had originally been carved from the surrounding rock-like coral, he requested that Mrs Clarke should still be interred there. Once that had been done, Lord Combermere ordered that sea-sand be liberally sprinkled on the floor to betray any intruders by the marks they left in it, and that the heavy door of the vault should again be cemented in place. This act was completed by him and his aides impressing their ring seals in the damp cement. No entry into the tomb could now possibly take place without the trespassers leaving unmistakable signs of their action.

But the official sealing of the tomb, as might be expected, resulted as time went by in a growing clamour among the island's population to have it re-opened, so its interior might be inspected to see what, if anything, had happened. Lord Combermere, as Governor, finally agreed to this being done on Tuesday, 18 April 1820, or nine months and one day after the final interment.

Sir Stapleton Cotton, later Lord Cambermere, battled Napoleon's troops in Spain before taking on the strange disturbances

He therefore met with Bowcher Clarke, who owned a plantation beside Christ Church and whose late wife had been the last corpse to be interred within the vault, and who, like him, was keen to know if any criminal ingress had been made into it. They next, along with several other eminent personages, one of whom was the Reverend Thomas Orderson, rector of Christ Church, went to the vault to effect an entry, watched by a massive crowd.

'Barbadoes has seldom witnessed such a gathering as that assembled in Christ Church district on that day,' wrote Mary, Viscountess Combermere in the biography of her husband. 'The towns were deserted, and thousands hastened to the scene; every spot, every avenue, every foot of ground was crowded in and around the churchyard ... and the old church standing forth in sombre relief, as if a connecting ink between the living and the dead, made the scene altogether one which beggared description, while perhaps its peculiar interest was in the death-like stillness that reigned over it – the silence of mute anxiety and superstitious awe.'

The entrance to the vault was not found to have been tampered with in any way, and yet it was only with great difficulty that the Barbadians employed at the task managed partially to open its sealed door. This was because a massive coffin within had been upended against it, which allowed only a narrow gap to be available for squeezing through, but once inside the sight which met the Governor's and his companions' eyes proved beyond any doubt that some force beyond the power and comprehension of Man had been at work. The sea-sand showed no scuff marks whatsoever, but all the coffins with the exception, oddly enough, of that of Mrs Goddard, the vault's first occupant, which stood where it had been left leaning against the far wall, had been moved from their places; some had been upturned, and the heavy one previously mentioned, which contained Thomas Chase, had been topsy-turvily propped against the door, thereby making it almost impossible to open. The Governor and his party were presented with an astonishing and deeply troubling sight, and one that seemed totally inexplicable.

But if Lord Combermere could not understand what had happened, he quickly discussed the matter with the Chase family and came to a conclusion about what should be done. He divined that after so many previous displays of malignity, from whatever source, it would be grossly disrespectful to the tomb's dead residents to leave them where they were, for they would surely be mistreated just as badly again. He therefore ordered that each coffin should be found a new resting place and that the vault from then on be left untenanted. And that is what was done, so that the vault remains empty to this day, visited only by morbid sightseers and student investigators, a testimony to the power, or so it seems, of otherworldly malice.

As we have noted, the sunken vault in the Christ Church

burial ground, located on that picturesque Barbados headland, remained as quiet as a tomb should be until Dorcas Chase was buried there. Her interment took place on 6 July 1812, almost five years to the day after Mrs Thomasina Goddard had been laid to rest, followed eight months later by Mary Chase, a blameless infant.

It therefore seems entirely clear that the wraith of Dorcas Chase, a suicide victim, was responsible for the disgraceful disorder witnessed within the vault when it was opened to receive the coffin containing her father's corpse on 9 August 1812. Through her prior act of self-murder she had made herself into a 'soul in crisis' after discovering that she had ended up in a far worse situation than the one from which she thought she was escaping. Indeed, it seems that she then found herself confined to the 77-square-foot area of that coral vault, with nowhere to go and nothing to see, and with nothing to vent her anger on other than the coffins entombed with her, notwithstanding the fact that one of them held an infant sister, albeit barely-remembered.

When another child (Samuel Brewster Ames) was interred in 1816 the same angry disorder was seen, as it was after the burials of Samuel Brewster, who was murdered, and Thomasina Clarke.

But as Colonel Thomas Chase was also a suicide, it seems likely that both he and Dorcas were responsible for all the later destructive behaviour, which included upending each other's coffins. When alive, he had been a plantation owner with a vile temper and a bad reputation, known for overworking and harshly treating his black slaves, and who evidently behaved equally tyrannically towards his wife and children. Dorcas feared him and was often driven to tears by him, which is why she reputedly ended her life by starving herself to death. Hence it is perhaps not surprising that both became souls in crisis when they realized they were incarcerated together in a small cell-like vault, ostensibly waiting for Judgement Day.

The two women named Thomasina who had had normal

deaths, like the two infants, would probably have gone straight to the next world, after perhaps a short sojourn in their familiar environments, as almost certainly would Samuel Brewster. As a victim of violent crime, he would not have been confined to the vault where his body lay, although he may have remained in the vicinity of his old home for a while before moving on, although there is no record of his wraith being seen there.

There is one interesting and relevant addendum to this fascinating mystery, which involves Lord Combermere, the only surviving son of Sir Robert Stapleton Cotton, Bart. Viscount Combermere, as he became in 1827, died at his ancient seat, Combermere Abbey, Cheshire, on Tuesday, 21 February 1865, at the venerable age of ninety-two.

In 1891 the photographer Sybell Corbet, a house guest at the Abbey, set up her camera in the library to capture a photograph of its interior, which obliged her to expose the photographic plate for almost one hour. The rest of the family and most of the servants were away together at the time. Hence she was not obliged to remain with the camera during this period. When the plate was eventually processed and a positive print obtained, it was noticed that on the very chair in the library in which the Viscount had liked to sit there appeared the form of an elderly gentleman, whose upper right half was clearly visible while the remainder was as invisible as a spirit should be.

Family members who saw the image testified that it was Viscount Combermere, whose ghostly presence suggests that he thereby wished to demonstrate, by making use of the opportunity the camera provided, the reality of the afterlife and *ipso facto* the genuineness of the events in Barbados. The fact that the spectre's right arm is discernible might refer to the fact that after the battle of Salamanca, Lieutenant-General Stapleton Cotton, as he was then, was badly wounded in his right arm by a Portuguese sniper and it was at first feared that the arm might have to be amputated. But he went on to recover from the injury, although his arm remained scarred and weakened for the rest of his life.

(Readers who are interested in ghost photographs may like to examine the photograph I took purely by chance of a phantom lady at Hadham Hall, Hertfordshire, in 1977. It can be viewed, along with that of a gruesome-looking demon, on the Ghosts' page of my website, midpop.com.)

It is helpful to compare the incidents in Burma and Barbados with the following remarkable poltergeist 'haunting' which occurred in Montreal, Quebec. I wrote an article for the *Montreal Gazette* newspaper about hauntings, which included the case, whose essence I reproduce here, when I lived in the 'Big Onion'. This gave me the opportunity to speak with one of the afflicted family members, although she was unwilling to meet me face to face (so we had to converse by telephone) or indeed to say much about it. The event had evidently been deeply troubling to the whole family at the time and had remained so after a hiatus of many years.

The strange case began in the summer of 1929 and the victims were a French-Canadian family living in a rented house on St Famille Street between Pine Avenue and Prince Arthur Street, not far from the downtown area of the city.

Quite suddenly and unexpectedly, much to the family's consternation, mysterious knots began to be tied in curtains, bed sheets and clothing, a process which continued and extended its sphere of operations until everything in the house that could be knotted was tied into small, tight knots.

'I said to my boss "That's a terrible thing",' the family member told me years later, when I asked her to recount what had happened, but who, even then, still wished to remain anonymous. 'And it was terrible. It put knots in everything. We 'ad to spend all our time undoing 'em. I wouldn't live in that 'ouse again for a million dollars. The spiritualists who came there said that somebody must 'ave cast a spell on the place'.

However, the knot tying still went on after the spiritualists had left, so the family asked two priests from nearby St Patrick's Church to bless the house. But unhappily, despite even their prayers, the knots continued to be tied.

When a bad smell unaccountably emanated from the basement, the police were called. There were fears that the body of a murder victim might have been buried there, whose ghost had resorted to knot tying as a way of drawing the family's attention to its presence. The police lifted the basement floor and probed and dug into the ground beneath it, but no body was found. And no identifiable source of the odour was discovered either, although the smell fortunately abated not long afterwards.

The police, showing remarkable presence of mind, then performed a test that was simple but revealing. They placed some ordinary, unknotted handkerchiefs and other items made of cloth in a room and then sealed it. A couple of days later when they unsealed and re-entered the room they found that all the items had been knotted, which clearly identified the strange phenomenon as genuine.

They next, without giving a reason, asked each member of the family to tie some knots, and by examining those produced they decided that the ones tied by the youngest child, a girl, matched those tied by the poltergeist. Hence they concluded that this girl had tied the knots unconsciously, which meant that she was the unwitting culprit. Their inference was seemingly verified shortly afterwards by the poltergeist activity ending as suddenly and as mysteriously as it had begun.

Yet while this finale apparently settled the matter, it was not the last heard of the St Famille Street phenomenon. For, when the tormented family had removed themselves to a new address, the next tenant to occupy the house was also bothered for a short time by something that liked tying knots. This threw doubt, of course, on the police's conclusion, but matters had by then run their natural course and further press interest could not be raised about the new development.

The only remaining explanation about the phenomenon which might be put forward is that an unknown spirit, yet one associated with the house, had taken a dislike to the family and had resorted to knot tying as a way of annoying them sufficiently to get them to leave. If so, it was entirely successful. It also seemingly vented its anger on their successors for a while, until it perhaps realized that they were not related.

There is also the disturbing and sad story of a woman who committed two murders and who afterwards killed herself, and whose ghost was later obliged to haunt the two houses successively inhabited by a lost nephew and his family, which included two daughters of about the same age as her own had been. For reasons of confidentiality I shall only use the Christian names of the people concerned.

The nephew, Henry, had had a troubled start in life because his mother died when he was a toddler, which resulted in his father marrying again. But when he also died, Henry was left entirely with his stepmother. She loved him, but as she was not prepared to suffer any interference from his own family, she moved with him right away from them, which meant that Henry grew up without having any contact with them or knowledge of them. They existed, in other words, entirely separately.

On attaining manhood, Henry met and fell in love with a woman named Dorrie and, although his possessive stepmother did everything she could to throw a spanner in the works, their marriage nevertheless went ahead. They eventually had three children, two girls and a boy. Dorrie was distinguished by the fact that she was a natural and talented psychic; she had known from the age of four that she could see people when others could not, which made it difficult for her to decide what hand to shake when she was introduced to other people's friends, as she often saw two or three perfectly life-like companions with them. Her gift probably meant that she perceived the wraiths of family members and associates who were spending time with their living loved ones after they themselves had died.

Young children are far more attuned to the presence of these otherwise invisible people but are usually told off for being 'too imaginative' or castigated as being 'liars' when they make such claims. I remember a certain Mrs Mepham, a duplex resident of Verdun, Quebec, telling me that 'On several occasions my three-year-old daughter has asked me "Who's that standing in the hall?" Once she said, "Who's that man?" I looked of course but there's been nobody there.' Yet psychic researchers have noted that the descriptions of the people children say they see often closely match the former appearance of local residents who died before they were born and about whom, ordinarily, they would have known nothing.

Anyhow, at their house in Surrey, Dorrie one day psychically perceived a scene which showed a woman in great anguish. Then one night not long afterwards, both she and Henry, who normally had no psychic ability, heard the sound of children's feet scampering along the upstairs corridor running between the bathroom and the bedroom. But when they hurried upstairs to find out what was going on they were met with silence, and on looking into the children's bedrooms they were surprised to discover that they were genuinely fast asleep. Hence they had not been responsible for the activity. After this took place on several other nights, Dorrie saw her psychic 'window' containing the unknown weeping woman widen until it reached down to her feet, where lay two dead girl children. She realized that they may once have been the scurrying children that she and her husband had heard.

Next there came an evening when the unseen children's pattering feet sounded particularly loudly and Dorrie and Henry hurried upstairs again to check what was happening. When they reached the landing they were horrified to find that there was water trickling down its wall. They rushed into the bathroom, but found that all the taps were turned off, so the source was not there. As before, the children were fast asleep in bed. Further investigation revealed no interior origin of the water from, say, a split pipe; the water in fact seemed to be emerging from, and be entirely confined to, the landing wall itself. It had to be dried with towels and cloths until it stopped flowing of its own accord. These odd happenings made Dorrie and Henry decide to sell the house and move to Brighton, where they hoped the sea air and change of scenery would alter the psychic atmosphere.

However, it did not. Not long after they had moved, Dorrie again began to receive psychic pictures of the woman who was in terrible anguish, which distressed her because she thought they had left her behind at the other house. And then one day her youngest child asked, 'Mummy, who is the lady who comes to sit on Lynne's bed and cries all the time?' Soon afterwards Dorrie and Henry started to hear their two girls talking and laughing, as if to someone else, in their bedroom after they had been put to bed and when they should be asleep. On going up to remonstrate with them, the nonplussed parents were told 'but we're only trying to cheer the lady up'. Which lady? their parents wanted to know. The answer, as Dorrie immediately realized, was not entirely unexpected. 'Why,' Lynne replied, 'the lady who comes to sit on my bed and who cries and cries.' When she was questioned further about her, Lynne told her parents that they had both for some considerable time been seeing and talking to the woman, and that they had, like their mother before them, taken it as a normal part of life to see people that others could not.

These apparent meetings between the daughters and the mysterious sobbing woman happened several more times which, while not alarming to the girls, was brought to a climax one night when Lynne, the eldest, was found sitting on the stairs, rocking herself to and fro, as if in anguish, lamenting 'I should be behind bars for what I've done!' Realizing that the woman had overstepped the mark by entering Lynne, Dorrie and Henry contacted their Brighton clergyman and arranged for an exorcism to be conducted. This was done and, while traumatic for the family, it did bring about the result they wanted, as Dorrie saw the woman's ghost manifest in the children's bedroom, float up into the air, and then go out through the window. It was not seen again.

And, thankfully, the answer to the strange haunting was determined shortly afterwards when Henry, who had been trying to trace his former family, managed to track down an old aunt. They corresponded and she in due course came to visit them, bringing with her a photograph album. The aunt was turning the pages of the album for them, when suddenly Lynne, pointing to one particular photograph, called out, 'Mummy, there's the lady who used to sit on my bed!' and Dorrie too recognized her as the woman she had been shown in her psychic visions. The aunt later revealed that she was a married sister of hers, who after the birth of her second child, a daughter like the first, had developed 'mental troubles' or what would today be called severe post-natal depression, and had, whilst bathing them, drowned both girls in the bath water. She was found to be of unsound mind and was given psychiatric treatment, but she could not cope with the enormity of what she had done and eventually committed suicide.

So the aunt's wraith had left her dead body with three strikes against it: the murder of her two children and also of herself, which made her a soul in crisis. She was henceforth obliged to remain here, unable to progress in the next world, until some resolution had been made. A link was established with Dorrie through Henry, and then with their two girl children, to whom she was able to appear and express her deep anguish and regret, and from whom she was in due course released by the rite of exorcism. The act of true contrition is the first step to asking for and receiving forgiveness, which she would doubtless gain in the next world, for our Lord has said: 'He that repents will be forgiven.'

This was and remains a fascinating case, which amply demonstrates that often the wraith or ghost which has committed some enormity cannot vacate the world as and when it likes, but must remain in exile here, alone and untended, until it finds someone to whom it becomes a reality and to whom it can express its regret and remorse. Initially we are all, it seems, obliged to judge ourselves, and the person who finds himself or herself wanting must expect to pay the price.

The case also has an interesting and unexpected dénouement, for not long after the exorcism of the weeping lady, Dorrie and Henry had two friends down to stay from London. The friends, looking somewhat embarrassed, told them: 'This may sound mad, but Mr and Mrs Egerton [not their real name, but people Dorrie did not know] went to a séance the other day, and were given a message for us "to pass on to someone in Brighton". The message came from a woman in the spirit world, who said that she is happy now and has been allowed to join her children at last.'

The last case I want to discuss briefly is perhaps the most frightening and inexplicable of all. It happened to the late Elsie Harrison, who died in 1998, when she was a young woman of about nineteen years of age and was living with her parents in a bungalow at Chelsfield, in Kent.

Early one morning as she suddenly woke up, Elsie noticed something moving outside her bedroom window, and she saw, to her alarm, a very dirty-looking woman, dressed in filthy rags and with hair wildly uncombed, who can best be summed up by the descriptive phrase of 'old hag', trying to get into the house through the door of the lean-to beside the bungalow. This door was fully visible from Elsie's bedroom window and was, as she knew, always locked by her father before they all went to bed at night.

But nonetheless, as Elsie watched, scarcely believing what she was seeing, the ancient crone somehow opened the door and let herself in. Moments later the woman came silently rushing into Elsie's bedroom and, without so much as a by-your-leave, climbed into bed with her. Elsie vividly remembered the weight and coldness of her body, the revolting smell she emitted, the rough feel of her torn rags, and the touching of her claw-like hands as the crone reached out and tried to maul her. Elsie was beside herself with terror at the pawing presence of this awful woman, for the whole thing was so sudden, bizarre and horrible. Uttering a scream of terror and loathing, she wrenched herself from the creature's bony grasp, flung herself out of bed and out of her room, and ran into her parents' bedroom.

Her parents were almost as startled when they were woken by their distraught and tearful daughter as Elsie had been at the sight of the old hag. Elsie's father of course went straight to her bedroom on hearing what had happened there but, alas, there was no sign of the hag at all. The rest of the bungalow was quickly searched but without finding the apparent intruder and, most disturbing of all, at least from Elsie's point of view, was the fact that the back door leading into the lean-to was still locked with its key still in the inside keyhole, so that nobody could possibly have come through it even if they had wanted to. So although the Harrison parents could see that their daughter was very distressed by what she said had happened to her, they could only explain it by concluding that she must have had a dreadful nightmare. Yet Elsie knew that she had been fully awake at the time and that the crone had somehow entered the house through the back door and had really climbed into bed with her.

Indeed, her ghastly experience was so vivid and terrifying that Elsie was not only delighted when she and her parents finally moved from the bungalow, but was imbued with a loathing of dirty people and of dirt in particular all her life.

It is difficult to know why Elsie was selected by the aged crone, if the woman was, as she certainly seems to have been, a phantom intruder. The incident only happened once and was not connected, as far as I know, with any preceding retributive action, such as a witch being drowned or burned. The woman might nevertheless have been such a victim and, if so, was therefore a soul in crisis – but this is speculative. So too is the notion that the hag might have been a succubus, which is a demonic female entity that enjoys ravishing the bodies of sleeping victims. This proposition is unlikely because Elsie was not asleep at the time and had not been wakened from sleep by the creature's groping, although both a soul in crisis and a succubus could disappear with the same rapidity as it did.

CHAPTER TWELVE

Animals, Cars and Aircraft

For that sweet soul's sake,
And for all sparrows' souls
Set in our bead-rolls,
Pater noster qui,
With an *Ave Mari!*

from *Phillip Sparrow* by the
Reverend John Skelton

EARLIER I DISCUSSED the remarkable psychic experience of Christoph Nicolai, the German bookseller and publisher, who during a difficult period in his life was able to see the wraiths and doubles of many men and women, some of whom he knew whilst others were complete strangers. Included in this remarkable array were men riding on horses, and also those accompanied by dogs and other unspecified animals. Birds were also seen. This in itself suggests that different creatures have an interior spirit, which not only can sometimes separate itself from their physical body during life but certainly does so at death.

Some people, however, have a problem accepting that other life forms might have a spirit that can continue beyond death and, although we must respect their viewpoint, they are almost certainly wrong. We humans, after all, write the holy books (with divine help) wherein these matters are discussed, and we are past masters at aggrandizing ourselves.

There are indeed many accounts from around the world of animal ghosts being seen. This in itself suggests that the phenomenon is a reality and not the product of fancy. The commonest sightings are of those animals which are most closely associated with us, with dogs topping the list, followed by cats and horses. That is not surprising, for when a strong emotional bond exists between an animal and a human, such as often occurs between a dog and its master or mistress, then that attachment is most likely to attract the animal's wraith into his or her presence after its death.

Some of the ghostly dogs that have been witnessed over the years are large and often black in colour, wherein they seem to act as forerunners to some disaster or of a death. But other canine apparitions are medium-sized to small ordinary dogs, which have no meaning attached to them except in so far as they inform the owners who lost them in death that they still exist. Such phantom animals inevitably have a comforting and reassuring effect on those who see or otherwise experience them.

Since becoming an adult I have only had one dog. She was a Great Pyrenees and she died, aged just over thirteen years, the year before my wife did. The breed is one of the largest, white in colour with characteristic *blaireau* (badger-like) markings on the head. I have often sensed her presence since her demise, but have not yet had the pleasure of seeing her, except in dreams, wherein my wife and she quite often jointly appear. It is heartening to know that they are together, for one does wonder what happens to a dead dog's soul when there is no one on the other side who knew and loved it when alive. This may mean, of course, that canine wraiths usually remain with their owners until one or other of them dies, notwithstanding the fact that they cannot normally be seen or even sensed by them.

Mrs Moore recounts the charming story of her hairdresser's little mongrel dog to which the young woman had become very attached during its life. It was white in colour and was distinguished by having a slightly deformed hip. The girl said that, although she had often sensed its presence after it had died, she tended to discount the reality of her feelings, preferring to believe that she was just being silly and sentimental.

But then, a year after the dog passed away, while she was with friends with whom she had been playing tennis, someone took a photograph of the group lined up together. They were all astonished when the film was developed because in that particular photograph the little dog could be seen, caught in mid-stride, looking as happy and as playful as it had been when alive. The film had somehow captured the image of its wraith, which was otherwise unseen by the human eye. The sight brought great comfort to the girl by affirming the reality of her feelings and showing that there certainly is a life beyond death for animals.

Another pertinent incident was recorded by Andrew Lang. Apparently a naval lieutenant once went to visit some friends in the country and when he arrived they were ensconced around a fire in the smoking room, accompanied by a fox terrier. Shortly after the officer had sat down to join them a large dog was heard slowly ascending the stairs, breathing hard, the clanking sound made by its collar clearly audible. The visitor knew immediately what dog it was and gladly cried out, 'Why, here's old Peter!', only to be corrected by the dog's owner, who laid his hand sadly on the other's shoulder, and said: 'Peter's dead!'

'The sounds passed through the closed door,' writes Lang. 'They pattered into the room: the fox terrier bristled up, growled, and pursued a viewless object across the carpet; from the hearth-rug sounded a shake, a jingle of a collar and the settling weight of a body collapsing into repose.'

The old but now dead dog had arrived in its wraith form to take its accustomed place by the fire, close to its master's feet, and who can be surprised (or fail to be delighted) at it doing so?

I have already related in Chapter Seven how my mother-in-law Emily, while she lived at an old rectory in Rutland, was once awakened in the night by the sound of a man and his dog entering her bedroom, both of which were ghosts. She heard the man divest himself of his coat and also the dog shake itself before it rambled around the room looking for somewhere suitable to lie. Like the dog mentioned above, it plonked itself down when it had found the right spot. This story too suggests that dead owners and their dogs find each other again and thereupon continue their existence together both here and in the next world.

Violet Tweedale, writing in *Ghosts I Have Seen*, recounts how she saw the wraith of her bulldog Pompey only ten days after he had died, walking just ahead of her as she went along a particular avenue in her extensive grounds. Delighted, she too called out his name, which unfortunately caused the wraith to disappear, for her suddenly focused attention doubtlessly directed her negative 'force-field' at it, so causing its dissolution.

When her second dearly loved dog, a collie named Triff, passed away, Mrs Tweedale felt its invisible presence by her for a long time afterwards, although sadly she never managed to see its wraith, unlike the butler, who saw it 'many times', and her maid, who glimpsed it twice.

Former East Finchley warden Barbara Mullins and her husband Brian were devoted to their two Yorkshire terriers, who lived for many years with them until their death from old age in the mid-1990s. Hence it is perhaps hardly surprising that the dogs can still make their presence felt in the quiet hours of the night.

'They were besotted with us, and because they used to sleep on our bed we could feel them pattering around quietly during the night,' Barbara recollected, thinking back to those happy times when the cheeky twosome were still alive.

'Then when they died, well, not long afterwards,' she went on, brushing a tear hurriedly from her cheek, 'sometimes when I'd wake up I could feel them walking around on the bed. Not every night, of course, but now and again they'd be there, and it does give you a little flutter. It just feels as though they're pitter-pattering across the bed. It's quite comforting really. I feel their little feet. There's a definite weight there too, as though they're there, creeping about.'

Barbara says that their visits sometimes happen when she's not always fully aware of them being there, for the tiredness of

*Deceased Yorkshire terriers Nicky and Kim visit
Barbara Mullins and her husband*

the day has claimed her, but that on other occasions 'It just hits
me and I think, "That could be them!".'

Barbara's experience is one that is familiar to many dog
owners who can often sense that their deceased canine chum is
still around. She has not seen her two former pets again, but
she has heard the brushing sound made by their feet and, as
quoted above, felt the weight of their bodies as they move
around on the bed. And it is quite in keeping with the behaviour of human wraiths to discover that the wraiths of dogs are
most active, or at least most easily discerned, during the hours
of darkness.

Yet, while it is generally true that the wraiths of dogs are most often seen, as opposed to being sensed, felt or heard, at night, there are many exceptions to this. I have already mentioned my own experience of seeing a woman walking with her small dog during an English summer afternoon, and David Lowsley saw a man out taking a morning walk with his dog. These incidents suggest that light is not necessarily an inhibiting factor where the apprehension of canine wraiths (or doubles) is concerned. Nevertheless the sighting of a canine wraith or ghost is a comparatively rare event, which is why such apparitions have entered the folklore of many countries.

However, before discussing the helpful appearances of those spiritual canines which act as protectors, I want to mention the dramatic sighting of a dog's ghost related by the late Thurlow Craig in his book *Animal Affinities with Man*, which happened when he was a cattle rancher in Paraguay. Craig wrote several books about his foreign exploits and the insights he had gained from working with horses and other animals. He later also contributed a regular column to the *Sunday Express* newspaper.

The occurrence in question took place in the unusually mild early spring of 1931, when the Welshman was working for an American company in the Chaco region of Paraguay. The snow in the nearby Andes had started to thaw prematurely, sending melt-water rushing down into the steadily rising rivers whose banks were soon broken, flooding the pastures on which cattle had been wintering. Craig and his fellow cowboys were therefore obliged hurriedly to move thousands of cattle, which had been trapped on the river pastures, in barges from one side of the swollen Rio Alto river to the unflooded eastern bank. The work involved confining the steers in holding pens before driving them on to the barges. It was slow and exhausting work, but vital to prevent a mass drowning of the distressed animals.

As the last load of cattle was being transferred that night to a barge, Thurlow Craig wheeled his horse around in the one-foot deep water to latch the gate through which the stock had just emerged. But at that moment the horse shied away, whinnied, and attempted to rear. Craig knew immediately that something had frightened the animal and, as he battled to bring it under control, he suddenly saw what he describes as 'a monstrous, brindled dog' walking away from the gate.

Clutching the reins with one hand, Craig immediately drew out his powerful revolver with the other, for lone dogs were not only often a source of rabies, but were likely to be calf killers as calves were easy meat for them. He then discharged two shots at the dog, certain that he would hit, and probably kill, the animal, which was no more than ten yards away.

Yet, when the gunsmoke cleared, Craig was startled to see no sign of the dog anywhere, either nearby or in the distance, for the moonlit night gave good visibility out over the surrounding shallow water, to a distance of about eighty yards. And the canine could not possibly have run so far in such a short time in water one foot deep. It had, in fact, simply disappeared. What on earth, wondered Craig, was going on?

The answer was provided when one of Craig's fellow cowpokes, who were all Paraguayan, asked him why he had fired his gun, and was told about the suddenly vanishing big dog. From his description of the creature, the cowpoke responded by saying that it was definitely not of this world, for it had been seen in the area several times before and was the ghost of a great dog which had been killed in 1910 when trying to defend its mistress from a brutal attack made on her by her drunken partner. The dog, which had been shot three times, was found lying across the body of the woman, who had died from the blows meted out to her, while the man lay dead some yards away with his throat ripped out.

So the gallant massive dog was cremated within the dilapidated shack where the couple had lived, while the couple themselves were buried in the local cemetery – apart, naturally. A grim story of drunkenness, anger and violence, but also one of canine courage and faithfulness.

'It was the first and only ghost that I have ever seen,'

comments Craig, 'but from then onward I knew to my perfect satisfaction that animals possess something which is part of them in life and which lives on after they die. I must admit that up to this turning-point I had had serious doubts ... but now I had seen for myself.'

Peggy Sullivan had a similar, if somewhat longer, meeting with a canine wraith one morning in 1966, when she was out walking her two dogs. The encounter was directly related to the fact that in the previous couple of years she had often crossed paths with another lady, who was likewise out with her pooch, which was an elderly Jack Russell terrier, and they would both stop and pass the time of day. These short chats usually occurred when they met in the fairly narrow lane or twitten (a local dialect term) joining their two roads.

Peggy had been somewhat surprised not to have seen her friend out with the Jack Russell for several days, which led her to wonder what had happened to them. So she was pleased one day to see the Jack Russell coming down the twitten towards

A neighbour's dog once vanished in front
of Peggy Sullivan

her and her two dogs, although it appeared to be out on its own, which was unusual. The dog was perfectly recognizable to her, and it was sniffing and snuffling as carefully as it always did. Her own two dogs, however, were hanging back and seemed reluctant to proceed along the path, despite them liking and getting on well with the Jack Russell.

As the little dog came nearer, Peggy stopped and leaned down towards it and extended her hand, calling out its name and then a friendly greeting. The dog, which was somewhat deaf, seemed to hear her for it too stopped and looked in her direction. The dog and Peggy were at that moment about five feet apart. But then, without so much as a friendly goodbye yap, the dog literally vanished before her eyes. It was, as she said, there one moment and gone the next, much to her astonishment. So she stood staring, trying to absorb what had happened. She was then roused from her stupor by one of her own dogs giving a sudden bark, and then both came tentatively forward as if ready to continue their walk. And so they all went on, but without their previous zest.

Peggy eventually found out the reason for the Jack Russell's disappearance. The little dog, she learned, had died one week before she had seen it alone in the twitten. Its mistress was then still recovering from the shock and sadness of its death, which explained why Peggy had not met up with her at all. Yet her dog had evidently decided to take an outing in wraith form along the familiar lane, which was when Peggy and her two dogs encountered it. But, once she had called to the dog and bent to offer it a hand, it was evidently time for it to go, hence the disappearance into thin air. Wraiths, as we have noted, often find it difficult to maintain their integrity when a person's attention is directed at them.

The famous Second World War airman Guy Gibson VC, who was killed in 1943 while taking part in the Dambuster raid, had a close bond with his black Labrador dog named Nigger. The dog would always watch as Gibson took off on a raid and be there waiting by the Scampton Airport runway to welcome him

A spectral Guy Gibson and his dog
were seen by a girl

home again. It was therefore particularly poignant and significant when Nigger was killed in a road accident on the evening of Saturday, 15 May 1943, which was the day before his master set out to drop the bouncing bomb on the Ruhr dams, from which he never returned.

In 1987 a memorial dedicated to Guy Gibson was unveiled at Woodall Spa in Lincolnshire and, after the church service the headmaster of the local school, whose choir had sung at the service, asked for a photograph to be taken of the children posing in front of the new memorial. The assembling group of choristers was unaccountably joined by a black Labrador dog that resisted all efforts to shoo it away and which was included in the final photograph, sitting in the exact middle of the group and staring straight at the camera. Nobody knew who owned the dog or where it had come from, and the animal ran off and disappeared when the picture had been taken. Nor has it been seen since. Only later was it recalled that Gibson had owned a black Labrador dog, whose visiting ghost the boldly insistent canine might therefore have been.

The notion that Gibson and his pet were reunited in death is further revealed by the several sightings of the pair had by a seven-year-old girl, who lived with her parents at the former Lincolnshire home of the pilot some years after his tragic death. The incidents were reported by Claire Cheshire, who knew her.

'She used to wake up in the middle of the night', Claire revealed, 'and see a figure dressed in uniform standing next to the bed of her little sister. Seated obediently at the feet of the figure was a black dog.'

From the child's description of the uniform worn by the unknown but very solid-looking man, who was not at all frightening to her, as neither was the dog, her parents determined it was that of a war-time RAF officer and that the twosome were almost certainly Guy Gibson and Nigger. The girl had no knowledge of military uniforms or of Guy Gibson. But, as I have pointed out, wraiths and ghosts not only like standing beside or at the end of beds, they are also more easily apprehended by children, who are psychically sensitive to their presence.

Black dogs which suddenly appear and then disappear have been reported from many parts of the world. They are, however, particularly common in Britain, which accounts for the frequency of pubs bearing that name. Almost every English county can boast at least one ghostly black dog that rambles within its borders, reports of which may date back for several hundred years. These mysterious canines are invariably described as being of a large size and jet in colour, with thick, shaggy coats and, most strikingly, if these are present, glowing red eyes. Yet while the beasts are formidable in aspect they are seldom harmful, although they may sometimes act as a forerunner of an accident about to happen to the percipient, or of his or her death.

Joan Forman relates the case of a Cambridgeshire couple

who were out for a drive one summer afternoon in their vintage car, when from out of nowhere 'a huge black, wolf-like animal' jumped over the car bonnet, leaving an intense coldness in its wake and scaring the wits out of their own dog, which was on the back seat. The couple stopped and searched for tracks of the animal, which had run into some allotments, but without seeing any further sign of it. The sudden appearance of the strange beast was both frightening and completely baffling, but its passage was followed by the couple undergoing a crippling financial loss a few days later, while the husband shortly there-after developed a serious kidney complaint which eventually killed him.

Yet despite such unfortunate consequences, whereby a suddenly appearing black dog serves as an omen of distress rather than being the cause of it, the ghostly animals most commonly and comfortingly behave as guardian spirits, protecting lonely travellers from getting mugged or murdered, or stopping them from losing their way in lonely places.

Mrs Moore describes the remarkable story she heard when visiting some relatives in Worcestershire with her husband. Apparently not long before a jeweller had been required to deliver personally some valuable gemstones, a task which required him to walk to the depot through some lonely coun-tryside, for as it was wartime no other transportation was available. The companion he had hoped would be available to accompany him was unexpectedly called away at the last minute on some important business. He therefore had no choice but to deliver the gemstones on foot at the prearranged time.

He left feeling somewhat apprehensive about the journey ahead of him, but he had not walked far when seemingly from out of nowhere he was joined by a large friendly dog, which looked well fed and cared for, and which not only walked along-side him but could not be driven away. In fact the man was so impressed by the dog's size and behaviour that he resolved to give it a home if its owner could not be found.

With his new friend by his side, the valuable package was

safely delivered and the job done. Amazingly, the dog even walked back home with him, which gave the man the notion that he had been adopted by it, which fired his resolution to keep it.

However, when he arrived home and was greeted with relief by his anxious spouse, he immediately spun round to introduce her to his new-found protector, but discovered, to his dismay, that the dog had unaccountably vanished. There was no sign of it anywhere, and indeed, despite spending time both then and afterwards looking for it, the man never saw it again.

A day later he learned that two would-be thieves had been arrested by the police. They had initially been loitering in some bushes alongside his route intending to assault and rob him, perhaps even murder him if necessary, but had been deterred from doing so by the sight of his canine companion. This had forced them to follow at a safe distance, yet no opportunity had presented itself before they had been picked up by a police patrol. The would-be robbers had learned about the jewel delivery from an inside tip-off, and had been responsible for sending the man's colleague off on a bogus business trip, in order to leave him alone to face their criminal intentions. The big dog, however, had foiled their plans and so had saved the valuable jewels from being purloined and the man from violent assault or possible loss of life.

It is impossible to say where the dog came from but its sudden appearance at such a fraught time, and its disappearance after the danger was over, suggests that it had a spiritual origin, although the question of whether it was a dead dog's ghost or a spiritual creature *per se* must remain unanswerable.

One dog's wraith that was seen quite unexpectedly in a woman's kitchen was encountered there by the kitchen owner's daughter Margaret Moreham, both of whose parents were keen spiritualists and held a regular weekly circle in their home in Dagenham near London, which was attended by various like-minded friends. Margaret described the canine encounter in an issue of the magazine *Psi Researcher*.

Because she was working at the time as a civil servant in the City of London, Margaret would often not get home until after eight o'clock on the weekday evening when the spiritualist meeting was held. So, in order not to disturb those taking part, she walked around to the rear of the house and entered through the back door, which opened into the kitchen.

One evening Margaret, having arrived home tired after her day's work, put the kettle on to make herself a cup of tea, and began looking round in the kitchen for something to eat, for she was also hungry. It was then that she had a sudden surprise.

'I suddenly noticed a small mongrel dog,' she said. 'It was not ours, so, assuming it belonged to one of our visitors, I spoke to it kindly and offered it the freedom of the garden. But it seemed puzzled, then went through the kitchen door into the room where the sitters were, *even though the door was shut.*'

Margaret realized that the small dog was an apparition. So, when the meeting was over, she went into the room to see if she could find out why it had been there. She was told that one of the spirits which had come through that evening via the medium (as it had on several previous occasions) had been a coster-monger in life, who had been accidentally killed in a market fight. That senseless tragedy had killed his little mongrel chum too, for it had pined away for him and had died of grief.

Moreover, the costermonger had apparently not realized that he himself was dead, so he had remained 'earthbound' like so many other spirits, and it was only by visiting the spiritualist meetings, as he had been, and talking through the medium to the people there, that he learned that he no longer belonged to this plane of existence. In fact, his visit there that night was to thank those who had helped him come to that realization. And, as he had also by then forgiven the man who had unintention-ally brought his earthly life to an end, plus having regained the companionship of his dear little dog, he now understood and accepted what he had become and was ready to move on with his chum into the world of love and joy beyond.

But, just as the wraiths of dogs can sometimes directly appear to their owners or make other sensory contact with them, so they can also appear to them in their dreams, sometimes when danger threatens their sleeping owner. One of the best examples of such an event happened in the United States.

In 1980 Lady, the much-loved Labrador dog of Walter Manuel, a resident of Los Angeles, died. During the three weeks following Lady's death, the distressed owner dreamed of her four times. Each dream was pleasant in itself, yet unusual in that water formed a common thread. In the first dream Walter saw Lady swimming across a lake to retrieve a duck he had shot; in the second Lady was gambolling in the surf while the family was on holiday; in the third the dog was with him as he did some angling in a trout stream; and in the last Lady jumped into the swimming pool in the garden to collect a stick he had thrown into it for her.

Walter Manuel could understand why he had dreamed about his beloved Lady, but he was puzzled by the ever-present water. 'I wonder why this is?' he said bemusedly to his wife. 'There were so many other things that we did together.'

Four nights after the last dream, Walter again dreamed about the dog, except that this time, instead of seeing her, he only heard her frantically barking, just as she had once done when some prowlers had entered the garden. On that occasion Walter had jumped out of bed, grabbed his rifle and had gone quickly to the window to frighten them off.

The barking dream woke him and likewise had him dashing to the window, where he was stunned to see his two-year-old son Jason, dressed in his pyjamas, hovering unsteadily on the edge of the swimming pool and reaching out with childish glee to the bright reflection of the full moon in the water. A moment later, uttering a surprised cry, Jason fell in the pool. His horrified father raced downstairs and was fortunately able to haul the spluttering lad out of the water before he drowned. The dream had enabled Walter to save his son.

'Nothing will shake my conviction', Walter said afterwards, 'that, in some way which cannot be explained, Lady actually warned me of the danger. It is just what she would have done if she had been alive.'

The waking of Walter Manuel by the sound of his deceased dog barking, right at the time when such an alarm call was needed, indicates that the barking somehow came from the departed dog. The odds for coincidence being responsible are so impossibly high as to discount it, whereas to suggest that Walter's own precognitive ability was responsible for him waking up when he did is merely to substitute one paranormal explanation for another. And, besides, why would Walter's sleeping mind need to create the fantasy of his old dog barking to rouse him, when it could surely have woken him up by itself and then consciously prompted him to go to the window? Arguing for an alternative explanation is only done to discount the afterlife, which, however, is a reality for many other creatures besides human beings.

Cats, like dogs, are sensitive to the presence of visiting wraiths, and their love of rambling about during the hours of darkness perhaps means that they encounter more of them than the average person. And their own continuance after death has been frequently reported by their former owners. Yet my personal experience of living cats has been slight, and I must admit to have never knowingly encountered the wraith of one. Admittedly, at age seven, a presumed feline did jump on to my bed when I was alone in a holiday camp chalet, much to my consternation, and then proceed to walk slowly up the blanket towards my head, but as I kept myself wholly under the bedclothes throughout its investigative peregrinations I never did learn if it was alive or not. It had gone by the morning, thank goodness, so its presence must remain a mystery, although the window was open at the time!

The incident, however, reminds me of the far more curious encounter with a disappearing cat undergone by Mrs Riftah Brown and her husband when the couple, who were in Spain on business, stayed at an expensive hotel in Madrid early in 1998. The political situation at the time was tense, chiefly because of the heightened threat from ETA terrorists. The Browns had therefore been warned to keep their doors and windows locked, and their room was on the sixth floor.

Notwithstanding these precautions, as Mrs Brown fell into a deep sleep one night, she heard the sound of purring and 'felt a pawed animal walking across my chest and abdomen, like a heavy cat'. She did not, however, leap up with a scream, but rather contentedly presumed it was a dream and surrendered herself fully to the embrace of Somnus.

But, astonishingly, the next morning her husband Ian told her that he had woken up in the night, and that he had, spluttered a dumbfounded Mrs Brown, 'glanced across at my bed and saw a large white cat on top of me, and that when he looked at it, it snarled at him'. Rather surprisingly, Mr Brown did not attempt to engage himself further with the animal, but turned over and went back to sleep.

No cat was found anywhere in the suite the following morning, which suggests that the creature heard and felt by Mrs Brown, and seen and heard by her husband, was not of this world. They did not unfortunately attempt to discover if a departed large white cat had any connection with the room, so the nature of the manifestation itself, whether it was ghost or an independent spiritual form, must likewise stay a mystery.

It is not surprising that a cat which has passed over is frequently experienced climbing on to someone's bed at night. After all, cats are essentially nocturnal creatures by nature, having as they do excellent night vision and a silent tread, both of which are necessary for them to catch mice and other small mammals during the hours of darkness. This naturally predisposes them as wraiths or ghosts to appear at night, a predisposition heightened by the general tendency of wraiths towards nocturnal activity.

Joan Forman mentions the experiences of a couple named Lloyd, who lived for a time at the old gatehouse at Paxton Hall in Huntingdonshire, where they not only saw a ghost dressed in Victorian-style clothing, including, rather remarkably, a stovepipe hat, but they also smelled the odour of cigar smoke in an unused room.

They were also visited at the gatehouse by a ghostly cat. The spectre would jump on to Mrs Lloyd's bed in the middle of the night and walk around the eiderdown purring in a friendly manner but, when she switched on the light to admire the visiting feline and caress it, the cat was found not to be there. The living animal had apparently belonged to a schoolteacher who had resided there in the mid-nineteenth century. It is believed that the schoolteacher was the origin of the ghost clad in Victorian costume.

Horses are as sensitive as dogs and cats to the presence of the departed. This propensity came out strongly in the experience of Thurlow Craig in Paraguay, whose horse nearly bolted when it detected the presence of the ghostly great dog well before he did. Craig thought it was a living animal until he fired two bullets into it and discovered that it was not flesh and blood after all. The horse recognized its supernatural character immediately.

These large animals, like other animals, have within them a spiritual form which leaves their physical self at death and which may also be able to do so in life. Christoph Nicolai had several sightings of men riding horses when he found himself able to see doubles, wraiths and ghosts, and those mounted men that he knew to be dead would have surely ridden the ghosts of horses. However, it is difficult to be certain if the solid-looking form of a riderless horse which suddenly disappears has come from a living or from a dead animal, unless of course one is personally acquainted with the creature and knows its history.

Yet, because most horses are domesticated and are usually thereby associated with people, it is perhaps not surprising for them to be seen after death either mounted or drawing a vehicle. Given that they are non-living, the existence of vehicles in the afterlife may seem totally nonsensical, but when it is realized that every physical object, as I pointed out at length in *Doubles: The Enigma of the Second Self*, has an associated inner spiritual form, which can at times be seen apart from it, then the idea is by no means as bizarre as it sounds.

Personal observation has taught me that both I and other people possess an aura, which is our surrounding spiritual envelope, and I can see exactly the same thing around non-living objects. And, as many who have returned from the other side following a near-death experience report having seen houses and other buildings, musical instruments, various work tools, and other everyday implements there, it is not beyond supposition to assume that vehicles of different types exist there too, or can be mentally called upon to exist there.

The following case, which I first described in *Buried Alive*, certainly suggests as much. The incident occurred in 1988, when Hastings resident Ken Harrison (no relation of Elsie Harrison) had a hip-replacement operation. His incision wound, however, became infected and caused him to develop a fever which brought him to the brink of death.

At the height of the fever Ken, in his semi-conscious state, suddenly saw a brilliant light in the doorway of his hospital room, which extended out to him and seemed to gather him into it, so that he became aware of nothing else but the light.

Next he found himself, to his surprise, carrying a suitcase and scrambling up to the top of a railway embankment. When he reached the track a train came along and stopped beside him, so he opened a carriage door and climbed inside.

The carriage contained a lot of other passengers, none of whom Ken knew, but he nevertheless managed to find himself a seat. The train started moving again and almost immediately it entered a thick fog, which completely obscured the surrounding countryside. As this took place a ticket collector came along the centre aisle. He noticed Ken and asked to see his ticket, which Ken did not have. He was immediately told that he shouldn't be on the train and would have to get off. Startled by this, Ken plaintively replied: 'You can't turn me off into nowhere. Look, I'm going to see my mother and father. They'll vouch for me when I get to the end of the journey.' His plea evidently touched the ticket collector, for he smiled kindly at him and agreed to let him stay on board.

Not long afterwards they arrived at a station, on whose platform Ken was delighted to see his mother and father waiting for him. He then gladly clambered off the train and warmly embraced his parents, as they did him. Both had been dead for years but now seemed fully alive and well. Ken said to them: 'I've come to stay, but I've left Joyce and the girls at home.' To which his father, shaking his head, replied: 'Yes, son, but I'm sorry, it's not time.' Then both parents, to Ken's disappointment, turned and walked away from him. Moments later everything vanished, leaving a kind of space, Ken said, with a gate in the distance.

The next thing Ken knew was that he was back in his hospital bed, feeling decidedly unwell. He learned later that he had come within a whisker of dying and it had very much been touch and go for a while. It thus appears that during the crisis Ken was given the opportunity to meet with his parents on the other side and to learn that they were just as much alive in their spirit form as they had been here.

But, equally amazingly, Ken also learned that large complex machines like trains even exist over there. Or at least, so it seems!

Now back to horses.

One sunny afternoon in the mid-1960s, a botany student named Michael Higgins was driving by car through the Meon Valley in Hampshire, heading for Old Winchester Hill, where he intended doing some plant collecting. As he took a minor road up a gentle hill, admiring the view out towards Hambleton, he was astonished suddenly to notice that he was passing a coach drawn by four horses, which was rattling along on the other side of the fence, in the adjacent field.

'I could clearly see the driver and someone else in old-fashioned dress on the front seat, and at least one person at the rear, with a post horn in his hand,' he noted.

'My immediate reaction was that perhaps a film was being

made, or something of that sort. At the top of the hill, only a minute or two away, the road widened and I was able to stop, get out, and look back. But there was no sign of a coach or a track, just an ordinary grassy field.'

Michael Higgins had no explanation for why he saw the equipage from a former period of history, which just manifested from out of the blue and then was gone again a minute or so later. The coach attendants' lack of awareness of him suggests that they and the horses were ghosts of the long dead who momentarily became visible as they drove in their replica coach from one earthly spot to another.

A similar unexpected encounter with a horse-drawn vehicle that vanished took place many years earlier in the nineteenth century in the New Forest. It happened to a resident gentleman and politician named Hyndford, who was riding by horseback from his home at Burley, it is believed, towards Brockenhurst, a small town lying about five miles away to the east. He had, at the moment the incident took place, temporarily lost his bearings but not, one hopes, his marbles.

Arriving suddenly at a grassy glade, Mr Hyndford noticed a carriage passing by on the other side of the bushes at its border. As the equipage passed a gap between them it came into full and clear view. The vehicle was an old-fashioned family carriage with imitation wickerwork green-panelled sides. It was pulled by two horses, and the driver was of the age and bearing to surely be a trusted family servant. Seated within the carriage were two elderly ladies, one of whom wore a hat, the other a bonnet.

As the carriage went out of sight again, Mr Hyndford rode through the gap in pursuit of it, hoping that he might obtain some directions from the driver. However to his complete bewilderment he found that there was no sign of the carriage and its occupants, that the avenue they appeared to have been following ended in a thick, impenetrable growth of bracken forming a cul-de-sac, and that the grass over which the carriage was travelling bore no imprint of horseshoes, no scuff marks, nor indeed any wheel tracks.

Hence what had appeared to be so real and tangible to Mr Hyndford moments before had completely disappeared in the short time it took him to pass through the opening in pursuit. But, being a man who knew that perceptions can sometimes be mistaken, Hyndford returned to the place where he had first noticed the carriage and looked for anything in the area which might have suggested such a vehicle with its three occupants to him. Nothing of the kind, however, was in evidence. He therefore went on, totally baffled by what he had seen and none the wiser.

These two brief sightings of horse-drawn coaches, along with their drivers, attendants and passengers, clearly indicate that horses do have a life after death.

In his own description of the New Forest incident, however, Andrew Lang characterizes Mr Hyndford's experience as a 'subjective hallucination', despite the fact that all hallucinations, arising as they do spontaneously in the mind of the percipient, are *ipso facto* subjective. But it is difficult to understand why Mr Hyndford should hallucinate a horse-drawn vehicle bearing at least three people, when such ensembles were common in the nineteenth century. Furthermore, there is no evidence that either Hyndford or Higgins had ever had such a remarkable experience before or ever did again, which suggests that the experiences were supernatural and not mental aberrations.

That dogs, cats and horses are the animals most commonly seen after their death should not surprise us because they live in close proximity to us humans. But a whole variety of spectral animals have been seen from time to time, whose number includes cows, bulls, oxen, pigs, sheep, hares and, most astonishingly, bears. Yet bears were once quite common in England owing to the nefarious habit of bear-baiting, which was a common enjoyment, and some bear ghosts doubtlessly originate from those poor ill-used creatures.

Hence it is no surprise to note that a spectral bear was seen at the Tower of London in 1816. It lumbered up a flight of stairs towards a sentry who, perhaps understandably, tried to protect himself with his bayonet. The weapon, however, went right through the apparition, whereupon the advancing ghost bear walked through the sentry and disappeared. The sentry thereupon fell down in a fit and the following day died from the dreadful shock he had suffered.

Having earlier considered Ken Harrison's experience of riding aboard a phantom train in the next world and now two sightings of ghostly horse-drawn vehicles in this one, it is pertinent to give some attention to modern phantom vehicles. It seems wholly fantastic, of course, for cars, boats, trains and even aeroplanes to produce an apparition of themselves, but there are many reported appearances of them.

In modern times, as we know, it is rare for the wraith of an accident victim to need to draw attention to its own missing dead body, because in most cases that is usually found shortly after the tragedy takes place. But nevertheless something like that probably did happen in the early evening of Wednesday, 11 December 2002, when motorists travelling along the busy A3 highway at Burpham, near Guildford in Surrey, saw a car leave the road with its headlights full on and seemingly crash into the vegetation at the roadside.

The police were called by several passing motorists, and it wasn't long before a patrol car arrived at the scene. A search was straightway mounted but no car was at first discovered. Then, as more officers arrived to take part in the search, a badly smashed Vauxhall Astra was found nose down in the ditch flanking the road. The vehicle was almost completely obscured by trees and tangled vegetation, and it was positioned about twenty yards away from where the car was reported to have left the road.

But it quickly became clear (or so it seemed) that it could not be the same vehicle, for the wreck had obviously been there for a long time. Not only had vegetation grown over it but there was no petrol in the fuel tank and the battery was completely flat. The most convincing proof of its antiquity, however, was the decomposing body of its driver which was found inside it.

Yet, despite the search continuing the following day, no other vehicle was discovered, which led to the supposition that the car which had been seen and reported veering off the road with its headlights on was a phantom vehicle recapitulating its former trajectory in order to bring the corpse of its occupant to the attention of the authorities, and so have him brought home.

The dead driver turned out to be a 21-year-old man who was last seen alive in London on 16 July of that year. His family had reported his disappearance to the police but, because his whereabouts were completely unknown and they had no idea he was going to Surrey, no progress had been made in tracking him down. It had therefore probably taken the dead man's wraith, driving a simulacrum of the car in which he had been killed, to alert his fellow motorists, and thereby the police, to the location of his last resting place.

It was just under five months from the date of the accident to the discovery of the crashed vehicle with the victim inside it. This is not an excessively long time for a wraith to wait before appearing after its body's death, if it is remembered, as I pointed out earlier, that a sudden and unexpected demise usually results in the soul being left in a state of confusion for quite some time afterwards. Indeed, much longer periods have gone by before a wraith gets in contact with a loved one, even when a person's death is anticipated and when post-mortem pacts have been made by the dying and those they leave behind.

That the young man was able somehow to generate his car's double and then drive it off the road with its lights full on was a remarkable act and points to his strong desire, even after death, to resolve the mystery for the living. It surely means that, once he had become aware of what had happened to him, he found he was unable to 'get through' directly to his living relatives or friends and was therefore obliged to pin-point his dead body in the dramatic way that he did.

Phantom aircraft have also been reported from time to time flying over the places where actual aeroplanes once went down. Such sightings often involve Second World War bombers which crashed either on setting out or when returning home over cloud-covered upland territory. The location of air crash sites in wartime was also frequently hampered by their occurrence at night when black-outs were in force, by poor communications, and most particularly by the planes coming down in barren, boggy and unpopulated regions of England like the Yorkshire Moors.

A phantom car crash at night with the lights of the vehicle blazing is immediately noticed and reported, and in the case described above, the actual car and its dead driver were found during the subsequent search. Yet, when an even more dramatic apparent air crash occurred some years earlier, no such fortunate outcome resulted.

It was on Monday, 25 March 1997 that a propeller-driven plane was first noticed losing height by several witnesses, most of whom were out of doors looking skywards in the hope of spotting the Hale-Bopp comet, which was expected to be visible that night. Two or three of them actually caught sight of the aircraft as it flew only a few hundred feet above the village of High Bradfield. Not long afterwards the aeroplane seemingly crashed into the moors eight miles north-west of Sheffield, producing a fiery flash and an uprising cloud of thick black smoke.

The police and other emergency services were told of the disaster by a number of widely separated witnesses, which verifies its reality. An extensive search for the wreckage was quickly mounted involving over a hundred police officers and several tracker dogs, seven mountain rescue teams, two helicopters, and a mixed bag of volunteers, who together combed almost forty square miles of moor throughout the night and into the following day. But, because no wreckage was found nor any sign of a crash site, the very expensive hunt then had to be scaled down and finally abandoned.

It was the most costly of a long series of searches following some twenty phantom crashes in the same area involving a propeller-driven aeroplane, which has been identified on different occasions as either being an Avro Lancaster (a heavy four-engined bomber) or an American Dakota. Two ghost planes, of course, may be involved, appearing separately.

A previous ghostly crash occurred in daylight during April 1995, when a silent, low-flying, propeller-driven plane, which was possibly a Dakota and reportedly sufficiently dense to darken the sun as it passed overhead, came down in a nearby field. Yet when witnesses rushed to the spot there was no sign of any wreckage.

This has led many locals to believe, and the authorities eventually to accept, that no plane actually came down on that March night in 1997, despite all those reports to the contrary.

But what is perhaps most interesting is that a Royal Canadian Air Force Avro Lancaster bomber of 408 Squadron did crash on a moorland peak known as James's Thorn on Friday, 18 May 1945, killing its six crew members, and that a United States military Dakota likewise came down, with seven fatalities, at nearby Shelf Moor on Tuesday, 24 July of the same year. The Lancaster crash site is today marked by a commemorative plaque. However, while both crash sites were located at the time and all the bodies supposedly recovered, it is possible that the accidental nature of the crashes and their occurrence just after the end of the war, may have contributed to their supernatural repetition.

It is therefore likely that ghostly planes will continue to collide with those remote uplands until the deceased crews come to accept the unfairness of a death which prevented them from physically returning to their wives and families.

Or until the unreported body of a fellow crew member is finally found and brought home.

CHAPTER THIRTEEN

More Strange Happenings

Life is only bright when it proceedeth
Towards a truer, deeper Life above;
Human Love is sweetest when it leadeth
To a more divine and perfect Love.

from *Incompleteness* by Adelaide Proctor

I BEGAN THIS book by quoting some thoughts about the genuineness of ghosts put into the mouth of a character in Samuel Johnson's estimable novel *Rasselas*; I shall start this final chapter by quoting the great man himself, who tells us the details of a fascinating ghost story, which was recorded by his biographer James Boswell, and involved a member of Johnson's own family, his first cousin. The maiden name of Dr Johnson's mother Sarah was Ford, and Sarah's brother Cornelius, a well-known physician, was the father of the man in question. This man, Johnson's cousin, became the Reverend Mr Cornelius Ford, a good-natured but unfortunately licentious country parson. It is said that he is none other than the cleric prominently portrayed in the delightful satirical print by Hogarth entitled 'Modern Midnight Conversation'.

'He was my acquaintance and relation, my mother's nephew,' explains Johnson. 'He had purchased a living in the country, but not simoniacally [i.e. in order to practise as a parson, not for profit]. I never saw him but in the country. I have been told he was a man of great parts; very profligate, but I never heard he was impious.'

This short description of Parson Ford, as he was habitually known, leads Boswell to ask Johnson if there was not a story of his ghost having appeared.

'Sir, it was believed,' Johnson replies. 'A waiter at the Hummums, in which house Ford died, had been absent for some time, and returned, not knowing that Ford was dead. Going down into the cellar, according to the story, he met him; going down again, he met him a second time. When he came up, he asked some of the people of the house what Ford could be doing there. They told him Ford was dead. The waiter took a fever, in which he lay for some time. When he recovered he said he had a message to deliver to some women from Ford; but he was not to tell what, or to whom. He walked out; he was followed; but somewhere about St Paul's they lost him. He came back, and said he had delivered the message, and the women exclaimed, "Then we are all undone!" Dr [Thomas] Pellet, who was not a credulous man, inquired into the truth of this story, and he said the evidence was irresistible. My wife went to the Hummums (it is a place where people get themselves cupped). I believe she went with the intention to hear about this story of Ford. At first they were unwilling to tell her; but after they had talked to her, she came away satisfied that it was true. To be sure the man had a fever, and this vision may have been the beginning of it. But if the message to the women, and their behaviour upon it, were true as related, there was something supernatural. That rests upon his word, and there it remains.'

The return of Ford's wraith to the cellar, as opposed to another part of the establishment, presumably happened because it knew that that was where it could speak with the one person who had no idea it was a wraith. No fear was thus evoked, which allowed it to have a normal conversation with the waiter, despite the unusual surroundings. It was able to ask him to warn the women concerned of some danger they were in. This was agreed to and the waiter decently complied, notwithstanding the shock he received when he learned about Ford's prior death. A similar difficulty would have faced the wraith if it had approached the women directly, for they too would probably have fled screaming from it. And while we cannot know the reason for their alarm when they heard the news given to them, which perhaps arose from some scandalous behaviour involving them and the parson and his cronies, their being forewarned must have prepared them to a certain extent for any consequences. The deceased reprobate parson therefore did his best to help them, which in the circumstances was a noble and chivalrous act.

Much has been written in recent years about what happens to someone after death. Such accounts are based by and large upon the testimony of those who have recovered from a near-death experience or NDE. As the heart stops, the soul or wraith is set free from the body and thereby takes its first steps in the next world. When the heart is restarted, however, the soul is obliged to leave whatever balmy setting (which is frequently a meadow or garden) it has found itself in and return quickly to its body. It is quite often reluctant to do so, but finds nonetheless that it does not have any real choice in the matter.

The rejection of a wraith which must return to its body sometimes becomes the duty of a zealous dead relative, who on rare occasions may have to turn forcibly back even its welcoming party, whose presence the relative may see as a hindrance to the wraith's departure. When May Hearsey's mother, for example, became very ill after giving birth to her seventh child, it looked for a while as if she would not survive the experience.

'When she regained consciousness,' May wrote about her mother's brush with death, 'she told us that she had returned from the spirit world. Her dead sister and mother had taken her by the hand across a green meadow. Just as she was crossing the border her father suddenly appeared, hit her mother and sister with a stick, and told Ma Ma Lay to return to her husband and children.'

The above-mentioned unspecified border, which has been recalled in other accounts as taking the form of a wall, fence, river or similar barrier, represents the extreme edge of the physical world, passage beyond which renders it impossible for the wraith to return to its body.

May Hearsey had a similar encounter with death when giving birth to one of her children. Her labour was very long and diffi-cult, and was worsened by fever and by fits. She gradually lost consciousness as her body systems slowed down, yet it was her husband Neil and brother Reggie, sitting by her hospital bed and gripping her hand, who fortunately provided the help she needed to prevent her irreversible exit from the world.

'I could feel myself slipping away,' she wrote, 'and I can only describe it as a feeling that my spirit was leaving my body, and I was wandering aimlessly in a meadow, and in the distance I could make out my dead brothers Willie and Clarence. Just as I seemed to be slipping into a deep, dark ravine, I was aware of someone pulling at my hand and calling me to hang on. Dimly I realized that it was Neil and Reggie and that I was still alive. Again I became delirious.'

In her case the 'deep, dark ravine' will have been the border that she had to cross or tumble into, from which she was saved by the hand-holding arousal that her husband and brother provided. May Hearsey was in fact doubly lucky for, having then given birth to a daughter, she again became delirious and even managed to acquire sufficient strength to jump out of bed and run around on the hospital lawn. On being returned to bed, she was restrained with straps and given soporific injections to keep her quiet. Her heart stopped again, and the nurse in atten-dance informed Neil that she had died. Distraught, he rushed home to tell her mother and family what had happened, but the prognosis was premature, for May was not only resuscitated but was returned to health and strength.

In the 1960s Douglas Fairburn, as I shall call him, owned a caravan which he kept on a site near the coast between Bridport and Lyme Regis in Dorset. He would go there to stay in that lovely part of the country for holidays, as would, on occasions, other members of his family. From the pretty spot can be seen an uplift of land known locally as Golden Cap, so called because when the cloud and mist clear from its summit, it becomes caught by the sun to give a remarkable golden apex of light. Douglas's caravan (which he no longer owns) was also within convenient walking distance of several small villages, and as he loved English churches he often went out for the day on foot to visit one or other of them. But nothing, however, quite prepared him for the strange experience which he was privileged to undergo.

On the day of the ramble Douglas arrived at the delightful old church he had set out to see, but after having viewed its exterior he was disappointed to find that its door was locked. He accordingly made enquiries at a house nearby about possible entry, and was told that the key, in order to prevent thefts from the church, was kept by the verger, from whom it might nonetheless be borrowed. Douglas therefore tracked the verger down to his house in the village, explained his interest in old churches and told him that he would like to view the church's interior, and begged loan of the key from him, which was readily granted.

Despite the inconvenience of the search, Douglas knew that he had made the right decision when he swung back the ancient nail-studded door and entered the quiet fifteenth-century nave, to survey the empty wooden pews and look up at the many memorials to deceased villagers which lined the walls. At one end of the nave stood a lovely carved pulpit, from which numberless sermons had been delivered, beyond which was a cloth-draped altar with its golden cross and candlesticks. He inspected each part carefully and every holy recess. At the other end of the nave, hidden from view behind a wooden palisade, was the enclosure at the base of the tower from which the bells were rung. The door giving admittance to that was shut, and Douglas found himself wondering again if he would be able to enter it and look around inside.

Hardly had that thought entered his mind when the door was hurriedly opened and a man whose face was obscured by the door's shadow looked briefly out and beckoned extravagantly to him. Then he stepped back and disappeared from view. Douglas was naturally surprised by the man's sudden appearance, but quickly followed him, for he was pleased at the opportunity of being shown a part of the church which was normally out of view.

When Douglas went through the door into the base of the bell tower, he found that the man had evidently opened and passed through another door leading off from it, for he could hear the sound of his steps climbing the staircase within. Delighted by this extra prospect, which was something he had never expected or anticipated, Douglas took the man's cue and followed him up the steep stairs. He soon came within sight of him, for the stranger plodded steadfastly upwards, while Douglas, eager to keep up, was advancing rather more rapidly. The man, he noted, was dressed in a long black coat that reached down to below his knees and was trimmed with silver buttons, beneath which his calves were visible clothed in thick black stockings. On his feet were worn but shiny shoes. Douglas thought that his garb looked strangely old-fashioned but, as the man was entirely solid and real, he put his dress down to eccentricity rather than anything else. He tried to say one or two hurried pleasantries to him between breaths but, as no answer was forthcoming, he assumed that the effort of talking was too great for the man and that any conversation would therefore have to wait until they arrived at the top.

The stairs led to the bell chamber wherein was found a narrow dusty walkway that ran around the inside wall and thus around the five bells. The bells were ancient and decorated with various motifs and Latin words, and the bell ropes rose up to them through apertures in the floor. Douglas found himself following the dark-clothed man as he led him around the walkway, uttering gasps of interest and wonder as he surveyed the venerable scene, but without receiving a response from the unknown man, whose face he failed to catch a clear sight of because of the gloom, his forward position, and the intervening angles and bells.

Then, before he knew it, they were descending the stairs again, and the downward motion required Douglas to slow his pace and to concentrate on where he was putting his feet. His silent companion reached the ground before he did, and when Douglas arrived there he glimpsed him stepping through the wooden doorway leading to the nave. Douglas pulled shut the door through which they both had just emerged and, feeling somewhat out of breath, gazed around with interest at the bell tower's interior, noting the bell ropes looped around their respective hooks, the dark wooden panels, and the list of former campanologists who had successfully rung this or that peel.

But then something occurred that Douglas has never forgotten to this day, nor ever will. As he turned slowly around, his glance again fell upon the wall where the door leading to the tower steps should have been, except that now there was no door there. Douglas gazed dumbfoundedly at the spot, feeling a chill run through him. He could make out the faint outlines of where an opening through the wall had once been, but it had been bricked up and painted over long ago. He stepped back, unable to take in what he was seeing, turning to look around again, just in case he had been examining the wrong wall. But there was no mistake about where the doorway, which he had twice passed through, had formerly been positioned, or for that matter the solid wooden door which only moments before he had closed. They had, however, unaccountably vanished from sight. Gulping, he hastily followed after the mysterious stranger and stepped back into the nave. But to his surprise there was no one in sight. He walked quickly around the whole church but there was not a trace of him anywhere. The man had also disappeared.

The verger immediately noticed that Douglas was a different person when he returned the key to him. His cheek was pale and his hand trembled. His voice sounded hoarse as he asked:

'Who – who was the man in the church? I didn't know there'd be anybody in there.'

The verger studied him closely, his brow furrowing.

'There wasn't anybody in the church,' he replied, his voice ending in a brief gasp. 'How could there be? I had the key.'

'Yes, there was,' insisted Douglas. 'I met him. He wore an old-fashioned black frock-coat. He wanted to show me the bells, for which I was very grateful. He took me aloft into the tower. It's quite a climb up all those stairs, isn't it?'

The verger's curious stare sharpened. 'The b–bells haven't been used for years,' he stuttered. 'They're too unsafe to ring and w–we haven't the money for their repair. The entrance to the staircase leading up to them has been bricked off. N–nobody can go up there now.'

'Well, I did,' said Douglas, trying to sound convincing. 'But when the man led me back down both he and the doorway vanished. I don't know what happened to them and I–I can hardly believe it did, but they just w–went somehow.'

A slight smile momentarily creased the verger's face. Then he nodded his head and sighed. 'I'm sorry, Mr Fairburn, but – but you're not the first to whom that's happened. The man you met is a former vicar, except he died a couple of centuries ago. He haunts the church, you see, and he loves people to visit it. He must have known that, er, you were really keen to look around, and he wanted to oblige you. So you've been particularly honoured if he took you into the tower. That rarely happens. I think the last time it did was about thirty years ago. I should feel very glad if I was distinguished like that by him.'

And that is the story of what happened to Douglas Fairburn, impossible though it seems, in a remote Dorset church. He both met there and saw a very solid-looking apparition, which he took to be a living person, and which very kindly showed him a part of the building that is bricked off and impossible to see. Like many other apparitions, the deceased vicar's ghost kept its face and gaze away from Douglas's direct view, for as has been revealed earlier the ordinary 'friendly' ghost is repelled by direct scrutiny and by the mental force accompanying it.

The ghost did something which it was almost certainly not

allowed to do, to wit, it opened a door and led Douglas through a doorway that no longer exists. How this was accomplished is unknown, but it did mean that the laws of nature pertaining to our time were temporarily suspended, for Douglas was somehow conducted through the brickwork blocking the entrance to the stairs and so given passage through the former doorway. I have no idea if the original door still stands behind the bricks, but its past self must nonetheless be there, which is what the apparition seems to have opened. Hence it appears the ghost was somehow able to manipulate time and space in order to show Douglas what it wanted him to see.

Hence ghosts, as Douglas Fairburn's experience unequivocally affirms, do possess powers beyond the ordinary, which certainly enable them to appear and disappear at will and to pass through solid barriers; they are also encouraged to help the living. But the urge to bend the laws of nature on occasions must be difficult for them to resist, particularly when a loved one will be the beneficiary. The church ghost, however, went right over the top in its desire to be helpful and gave startling assistance to someone it had never encountered before.

We can only hazard a guess as to why it went out on a limb like that. It may of course have tired of working within the narrow constraints imposed on it, or it may simply have wanted to show off. Its lengthy earthbound residence in a remote country church suggests that it may be paying off some sort of psychic debt, or it may, of course, simply love being there and lack any desire to progress further in the next world. We simply don't know what its motives are or what boundaries are imposed on it. But it remains a helpful spectre *par excellence* and thus finds a rightful and welcome place in this book.

The reader will surely remember the frightening assault that Elsie Harrison experienced when she was a young woman of nineteen summers. Her dirty and repulsive assailant, who climbed into bed with her, was almost certainly the wraith of a gipsy woman, whose compatriots had been living and dying in the district for many years. The traumatic incident unfortunately gave Elsie a revulsion for dirty old women in general, who ever afterwards scared and disgusted her.

It is, however, important to emphasize that such happenings are rare. Most wraiths and ghosts, as we have seen, want only to help the living and should be counted as our friends. The few that can and do cause alarm and distress invariably originate from people who have either died in dreadful circumstances or whose lives were blighted in some way. They carry their bitterness and warped personalities with them, which makes it difficult for them to accept that they are dead or to make any progress in the next world, where help and comfort is always available to the soul in distress.

But it is heartening to report that Elsie had an earlier encounter with an unknown supernatural presence, which may have been a ghost, and which demonstrated the typically helpful and benign nature of most post-mortem contacts. The experience played an important part in moulding her adult likes and interests. And, by showing her a wonderful degree of kindness and compassion, it helped her to overcome the shock of the later assault.

When Elsie was a girl of about eight years old she lived with her family in the top two floors of an old and rather dismal Victorian villa in south-east London. She did not like the house very much, and she especially disliked a certain large cupboard built under the stairs leading up to the attic, which she had to pass every time she returned from school. Cupboards are seldom relished by young children, for they are seemingly the hiding places of all sorts of frightening creatures, and that cupboard was particularly scary because, when her mother had opened its door one day, the unexpected glimpse Elsie had of its very dark interior gave her the impression that it went on for ever.

Elsie's fear of the cupboard unaccountably grew as the days passed. She had to steel herself to pass it, which she invariably did at a run, and it made going out or coming home into something of an ordeal for her.

Her mother became increasingly worried about Elsie's state of mind and so-called childish anxiety but, by pondering deeply on the problem, she at last came up with what she thought was a sound way of curing her daughter of her unnatural terror. This was based on what today would be called reverse psychology. She resolved to take away the fear of the cupboard by removing the sheets and blankets kept inside it and replacing them with Elsie's toys and playthings, all of which she loved. But what her mother did not fully realize was that it wasn't the cupboard's contents that scared her daughter, but its dark cavernous interior and the unseen beings that doubtlessly lurked there.

The momentous change, however, was explained to Elsie when she returned from school that day and, despite her sobs, cries and protests, her mother took her by the hand, led her firmly to the cupboard, opened wide its door, and showed her all her dolls and other toys sitting quite unconcernedly on the shelves within. The message to her was plain: if they don't mind being in the cupboard, why should she mind going there? But the point was missed again. Every child knows that toys are brave; they don't mind the dark, and they don't even mind being played with by creepy things. But, notwithstanding Elsie's tears, her mother was adamant, and from then on if Elsie wanted a toy to play with she had to go to the cupboard and get it for herself. Even loving parents can sometimes be misguidedly cruel.

In the days that followed Elsie did as her mother asked. She went with a wildly beating heart and trembling hands to the dreaded door, quickly wrenched it open, snatched the doll or teddy bear she wished to play with, slammed the door shut again, and stamped her feet hard on the wooden floor as she ran back to safety with it, breathing hard. It soon became a regular performance, which while partly solving the problem did not cure Elsie of the fear she still felt towards the vast darkness within.

There then came a day when, after having coped with her terror for a while, Elsie felt sufficiently proud of herself to show her two younger brothers how brave and resolute she was. So she took each by the hand and led them to the awful door. The silence behind it was just as frightening to her as ever but, swallowing hard, Elsie released her grip on her siblings, took a firm grip of the door handle and, using all her strength, pulled open the door.

The sight that met her eyes took her breath away. For lying on the shelves which had become the dismal grandstand of her toys was a mass of lovely, varied, colourful flowers. They filled the space completely, masking off the darkness behind, which now seemed like a remote memory. Elsie gasped in wonderment as she gazed around at the beautiful blooms, whose brightness was enhanced by the ethereal light in which they were bathed. She recognized some of the flowers, like the tulips and roses, while others, even more beautiful, she had never seen before. It was a thrilling spectacle beyond her wildest dreams.

The magical display lifted her young heart. And, as she gazed delightedly around at the flowers, completely entranced by them, they suddenly shimmered and then slowly faded from view, to reveal her dolls, games and teddy bear still sitting behind them, while beyond lay the unfathomable darkness. But Elsie knew at that moment that the blooms had taken with them all the fear and disquiet she had felt before. She glanced excitedly down at her brothers, but they were reaching out only for the toys: for they had not, she realized, seen the flowers at all. The flowers had only been for her eyes.

We cannot know, as I mentioned earlier, what loving, thoughtful and helpful presence drove away that little girl's fright in such a marvellous way. It may have been a house ghost, or perhaps some higher spiritual being, like an angel. It performed a wonderful act of kindness which, if it was a spectre, it may not strictly have been allowed to do. But thank goodness it did, for it not only calmed Elsie's fears: it also gave her a love of flowers, plants and gardening, which remained with her all her life. She grew to see beauty in even the humblest groundsel; or as Christina Rossetti more roundly expressed it:

But not alone the fairest flowers:
The merest grass
Along the roadside where we pass,
Lichens and moss and sturdy weed,
Tell of His love who sends the dew,
The rain and sunshine too,
To nourish one small seed.

Yet, notwithstanding the great knowledge of plants and of their blooms which Elsie acquired during the course of her long life, and she lived until the age of ninety, she was never able to discover what those unknown transcendent flowers were that she was privileged to see in a dark cupboard in south-east London.

They were mayhap the flowers of Paradise.

Bibliography

Anonymous Churchman, *Apparitions, Supernatural Occurrences, Demonstrative of the Soul's Immortality* (J. Barker, London, 1799)

Augustine, St, *Concerning the City of God Against the Pagans* [translated by Henry Bettensen] (Penguin Books, 1977)

Barrett, Sir W. F., *Psychical Research* (Williams & Norgate, Ltd, 1911)

Boswell, James, *The Life of Samuel Johnson, LL.D.* (Office of the National Illustrated Library, 1857)

Bradley, H. Dennis, *... And After* (T. Werner Laurielly, 1931)

Bradley, H. Dennis, *The Reality of Physical Phenomena* (The Society of Communion, 1928)

Collier, Ron, *Dark Peak Aircraft Wrecks* (Wharncliffe Woodmoor, 1982)

Craig, Thurlow, *Animal Affinities with Man* (Country Life Limited, 1996)

Creighton, Helen, *Bluenose Ghosts* (Nimbus Publishing, 1994)

Davies, Rodney, *Disembodied Voices* (Robert Hale, 2000)

Davies, Rodney, *Doubles: The Enigma of the Second Self* (Robert Hale, 1998)

Davies, Rodney, *Journeys to Heaven and to Hell* (Robert Hale, 2002)

Davies, Rodney, *Supernatural Disappearances* (Robert Hale, 1995)

Dyall, Valentine, *Unsolved Mysteries* (Hutchinson & Co., 1954)

Forman, Joan, *Haunted East Anglia* (Fontana, 1976)

Gerald of Wales, *The Journey Through Wales/The Description of Wales* [translated by Lewis Thorpe] (Penguin Classics, 1988)

Haynes, Renée, *The Seeing Eye, The Seeing I* (Hutchinson, 1976)

Hearsey, May, *Land of Chindits and Rubies* (Mrs M.A. Leverston-Allen, 1981)

Hole, Christina, *Haunted England* (B.T. Batsford Ltd, 1951)

Hone, William, *Table Book* Volume 1 (Hunt and Clarke, 1828)

Johnson, Dr. Samuel, *The History of Rasselas, Prince of Abyssinia* (Bell & Bradfute, James M'Cliesh, William Blackwood, 1806)

Lang, Andrew, *The Book of Dreams and Ghosts* (Longmans, Green, and Co., 1897)

Mary, Viscountess Combermere and Capt. W. W. Knollys, *Memoirs and Correspondence of Field Marshall Viscount Combermere* (Hurst and Blackett, 1866)

Moore, Margaret Gordon, *Coincidence?* (Rider and Co., 1940)

Noble, Reverend Mark, *Biographical History of England* (H. Richardson, 1806)

Paranormal Review (Society for Psychical Research, various issues)

Psi Researcher (Society for Psychical Research, various issues)

St Aubyn, Astrid, with Zahra Hanbury, *Ghostly Encounters* (Robson Books, 1998)

Shank, Bradford, *Fragments* (Prentice-Hall Inc., undated)

Simpson, Reverend David, *A Discourse on Dreams and Night-Visions* (Edward Bayley, 1810)

The Unexplained: Mysteries of Time and Space (Orbis Publishing Ltd, 1980)

Tweedale, Violet, *Ghosts I Have Seen* (Herbert Jenkins, 1931)

Tyrrell, G.N.M., *The Personality of Man* (Pelican Books, 1947)

Index

aircraft, phantom, 207–9
Akerman, Jean, 96–7
Ames, Samuel Brewster, 169
...And After, 127
A Night in Venice, 16
Animal Affinities with Man, 189,
    190–1
animals, double and wraiths of, 40,
    184 passim
Anne, her experience, 117–18
apparitions, fear of, 9, 157, 158,
    159, 161, 197
aura, 12
Avro Lancaster, ghost of, 209

Bagnall, Dr, wraith of, 130
Bank of England, official's strange
    experience, 94
Barbadoes, 166 passim
Bardens, Dennis, 13, 18–19
Barnsbury, séance at, 26
Barrett, Sir W. F., 87
Beal, visit by mother's wraith, 45–6
bear, ghost of, 205–6
Bedessee, Radha, 137–8
Bell Hotel, spectre seen at, 33
Berry, Mr, frightening experience of,
    103–4
Blashford-Snell, John, ghostly experi-
    ence of, 37–8
Boswell, James, 93
Bower, Lieutenant Eldred W. Bowyer,
    59–61, 89, 90
    drawing of, 60
Bower, Florence Bowyer, son's
    appearance to, 89–90
Bowyer-Bower, Adèle, 61–2
Bowyer-Bower, Dr Tanya, 61
Boyce, Monica, experiences of,
    76–80, 95–6
    drawing of, 77
Bradley, H. Dennis, 124–7,

drawing of, 124
Brewster, Samuel, 170, 175
Brian and Anne-Marie, ghostly expe-
    rience of guest of, 30
Brown, Riftah, 199–200

Calignon, Soffrey de, 97–8
Campbell, Lieutenant A. B., 123
car, spectral, 206–7
cats, wraiths of, 199–201
Chase, Dorcas, 167–9, 174
Chase, Mary Anna Maria, 166
Chase, Colonel Thomas, 166, 167–8,
    169, 173, 174
Chater, Mrs Cicely, 61
Chater, Elizabeth, wraith seen by, 61
Cheshire, Claire, 194
Christ Church, 166
Cicero, 43
Clarke, Bowcher, 172
Clarke, Thomasina, 171
Collins, Brenda, experiences of,
    52–3, 108–9
Combermere, Lord, 171, 173, 175
    drawing of, 172
Combermere, Viscountess Mary,
    quoted, 172–3
contemplation, 24
Corbett, Sybell, 175
Corder, William, 146–8
    drawing of, 147
Corfidius brothers, strange affair of,
    133–4
Cotton, Sir Stapleton, drawing of,
    172
Craig, Thurlow, ghostly dog seen by,
    189–91, 201
Craven, Gemma, ghost seen by, 55
Creighton, Dr Helen, 88, 102, 130,
    142
Cripplegate, incident in, 144–6
Crowley, Aleister, 83

Dakota, ghost of, 209,
Dark Night of the Soul, the, 24
Davies, Rodney, ghostly experiences
of, 13–14, 23–4, 32, 35, 66,
106–8, 109–15, 127–8, 130–1,
140–1, 199
depression, 24
Dimbleby, Stephen, faceless ghost
seen by, 35–6
dogs
black, 194–5
ghosts of, 184, 185–99
Great Pyrenees, 185
doppelgänger, 13
doubles, 13 passim

Eaton, Jill, ghostly experiences of,
80–1, 84, 90–1, 105–6
Elgey, 2nd Lieutenant E., 59
Elizabeth, 63, 112
wraith seen by, 64–5
Elson, John, wife's wraith seen by,
128–9
Emily, strange experience of, 116–17

Fairburn, Douglas, remarkable expe-
rience of, 213–18
fetch, 25
Fisher, Frederick George, 152–7
Ford, Reverend Cornelius, wraith of,
210, 211
Ford, Sarah, 210
Forman, Joan, 194, 200–1
Frank, wraith of, 48–9
ghost of appears to sister, 49–52

Gerald of Wales, quoted, 52
Géricault, Théodore, ghost of, 71–2
ghost, 25 passim
Gibson, Guy, VC, 192–4
drawing of, 193
Goddard, Thomasina, 166, 168, 170
Golden Cap, 213
Gordon, Adam Lindsay, quoted, 154
Great Pyramid, 9
Greenwood, Elizabeth, dreams of,
145–6
Griggs, Reverend, 164

Hale–Bopp comet, 208

hallucination, 62
Harrison, Elsie, experiences of,
182–3, 218–22
Harrison, Ken, near-death experience
of, 202–3, 206
Hayes, Renée, 83
Hearsey, Clarence, 54–5, 161, 162
Hearsey, May, 84, 85,
quoted, 212, 213
Hearsey, William, ghost of appears
to son, 54–5
Hearsey, Willie, 162, 163–6
Hendry, M., nurse, strange experi-
ence of, 19
Henry, 178 et seq
Higgins, Michael, 203–4
Highett, Aeta, 90
Hobson, Elizabeth, 27–8, 44–5
Hone, William, 74
horses, ghosts of, 201
Household Words, quoted, 154–5,
157
Husk, Mr, double of, 26
Hyndford, Mr, 204–5

Imlac, 9–10

Jack Russell, wraith of, 191–2
Jim, warden, double seen by, 38
Johnson, Dr Samuel, 9, 10, 93, 210–12
Julian, Mother, 24

Keulemans, J. C., 26
Knutsford, incident near, 150–1

Lady, Labrador dog, 198–9
LaGrand, Louis, 98
Lang, Andrew, 16, 115, 186, 205
Laodice, 127
Laurentia, Acca, 136–7
Lett, Charles, 87
lights, mysterious, 26, 31
Lowsley, David, strange experiences
of, 66–8, 69–70, 189
Lustgarten, Edgar, 135
Lynne, 180, 181

Ma Ma Lay, 162, 163
manes, 25
Manuel, Walter, 198–9

Marang, Burma, 84
Martin, Maria, murder of, 146–7
Maymyo, Burma, 161
McCue, Iola, 84–7
    drawing of, 86
McCue, Neil, 84–5, 213
McCue, Reggie, 213
Megara, incident at, 143–7
Mepham, Mrs, 178–9
mist, appearances of, 103 et seq
Montanist, vision of, 12–13
Moore, Margaret Gordon, 34, 78,
    128
    quoted, 129, 185, 195
Moore, William, quoted, 158, 159
Moreham, Margaret, 196–7
Moreton, Samantha, strange experi-
    ence of, 99–100
Mullins, Barbara, 187–8
    drawing of, 188

near-death experiences (NDE), 23,
    25, 212
Nicholai, Christoph, extraordinary
    experience of, 39–42, 44, 184,
    201
Nigel B., 95

odours, spirit, 83 passim
Orderson, Reverend Thomas, 172
out-of-body experience, 14
Owen, Wilfred, poet, 57–9
    drawing of, 58

Pearson, Paul and Sylvia, 29, 100
Pekuah, 9, 10
Pellet, Dr Thomas, 211
Peterson, Charles, ghostly experi-
    ences of, 22, 28–9, 70–2
phongyi, 163
photographs of ghosts, 34, 175, 186
Pliny the Elder, 133
poltergeist, 31
    in Montreal, 176–7
Pryor, Martyn, 56–7
psychokinesis, 165
Pyrochles, quoted, 25

Rasselas, 9, 43
Rea, Thomas, wraith of, 27, 44

Rebecca, 101
R. G., 135–6
Romans, beliefs of, 25
Royal Masonic Hospital, 18

Sabine, Joseph, 46–8
St Augustine, 134–5, 136
St John of the Cross, 24
S. B., sees double of herself, 20–1
Shakespeare, William, quoted, 150
simulacrum, 65, 74, 132, 207
soul form, 12, 13, 16, 120
Spearman, Lady Dorothy, 59–60, 62
spirit light, 26
spirit, matter interpenetrated by, 69
Stenton, Lily, OBE, experiences of,
    15–16
Stratton, Albert and Alfred, 136
suicide, wraith of, 56
Sullivan, Peggy, 75, 191–2
    drawing of, 191
Supernatural Disappearances, 65, 66,
    155

telepathy, 62, 63
Tertullian, Quintus, 12
Thomas, John, 158–9
Towns, Captain, 87–8
Tweedale, Violet, 187

unseen presence, 74 et seq

Valiantine, George, 125–6, 127
Varro, Marcus Terentius, 133
vault, disturbances in, 166 passim
    drawing of, 167
Versatile Monahans, the, 16, 76
voices, 93 passim
Voss, Lieutenant Werner, 59

Walter, 32, 33
Wesley, John, 27
W., Mary, 55–6
Women's Royal Naval Service
    (WRENS), 78
Wontner, Harry, 34
Worral, George, 153, 156, 157
Worth, Sally, 16–18, 104–5, 117
wraith, 25 passim, 28, 43, 126
Wratten, Dorothy, 94